The Broken Line

Christopher Schuring

ISBN: 979-8-89525-333-5

Dedication

This book is dedicated to the many individuals and organizations who have contributed, both directly and indirectly, to its creation. To those who provided their creative insight, offered valuable information, and shared their expertise, I extend my deepest gratitude. Your guidance and support shaped the foundation of this work and allowed it to flourish.

Special thanks go to the numerous business leaders, innovators, and organizations involved in this process. Your experience and willingness to share your journeys enriched the content in ways that I could not have achieved alone. You provided not just facts and figures but also wisdom and inspiration, which I hope will resonate deeply with the readers of this book.

However, this dedication is not solely for those who helped. It is also for those who stood as obstacles along the way—the ones who, through opposition or indifference, created the trials and tribulations that are an inevitable part of any entrepreneurial journey. To the gatekeepers, the naysayers, and those who cast doubt on the dreams of startups and founders, this book is for you as well. In many ways, it is because of you that this work came to be. The challenges you presented pushed us to think more deeply, work harder, and become more resilient. Without such resistance, the spirit of innovation would not burn as brightly.

This book is, therefore, a testament to the dual forces at play in the world of entrepreneurship: those who lift and those who limit. Both are essential. The process of building something new is never a smooth path, and often, it is the very obstacles that sharpen our resolve, force us to innovate, and refine our ideas.

I hope that everyone who reads these pages—whether they are leaders, entrepreneurs, or aspiring founders—finds in them the tools to overcome the hurdles that lie ahead. My wish is that the words within this book can, in some small way, help to reduce the trials and tribulations faced by those who dare to dream, build, and create.

To those who support you and those who stand in the way, this book is for you. You have each played a role in its creation, and I am grateful for that. Thank you for being part of this journey, whether you intended to be or not.

Acknowledgment

I am deeply grateful to my wife of 43 years, my numerous business partners, and everyone involved in my various startups. Your unwavering support, hard work, and resilience in the face of startup funding challenges have been invaluable. Without your efforts, this book would not have been possible, and I might still be working in a warehouse somewhere—probably trying to figure out how to turn a forklift into a startup.

About the Author

Let's begin this adventure with a bit of background as it relates to Chris Schuring, the author of this little diatribe.

We'll start the adventure with some background on the author's experiences, failures, and insights related to seeking investments, starting companies, and taking them to the next level.

The author has a rich and diverse background in entrepreneurship and startups, which entails participating in and leading capital-raising and budget-handling tasks. They have experienced the highs and lows of the entrepreneurial journey, gaining valuable insights along the way.

With an extensive 50-year career in the technology and sales fields and advancement into executive management and business ownership, Christopher Schuring has been involved in business ranging from meat processing to international data center management for the emerging web-based enterprises of the 1990s. He also has experience in the carbon industry: *algae for carbon capture and storage.*

Through these experiences, he was able to gather a wealth of knowledge in the real world, facing real-world scenarios.

This made it possible for Schuring to achieve high-level management positions at several startup firms in strategic, tactical, sales, and marketing areas. He went on to become a consultant and held a position on the TAB (Technical

Advisory Board) and Board positions with several companies.

This led to Schuring having multiple businesses in the energy and energy consulting fields, allowing him to have experience in international business in Korea, Japan, the United Kingdom, Germany, China, India, Guatemala, West Africa, New York, and California.

Schuring moved on to become a motivational speaker for sales organizations for five years. He owned an internet-based radio station that had over 7,000 listeners a week being broadcast in 35 countries. He conducted media interviews with NBC, CBS, CNBC, CNET, The Family Channel, Greta Wire, SMUD TV, newspapers, radio program hosts, and on-air personalities. He also had over 550 hours of talk time on various AM, FM, and Blog talk radio shows on the subject of solar energy.

He has been a founder or partner in organizations from Landscaping to International Data Centers and POP operations.

Many other activities have led to the formation of this book, some of which we will explore in the chapters that follow.

Preface

"The supreme art of war is to subdue the enemy without fighting."

-Sun Tzu

In military terminology, a *"broken line"* typically refers to a graphical representation on a map or operational plan that indicates a portion of a defensive or offensive line that is not continuous. It is often used to depict areas where the line of defense or attack is interrupted, allowing for flexibility in the positioning of forces or indicating areas of reduced emphasis.

We are experiencing the Broken Line; our defenses and our offenses are not together. The process of funding and starting a business is set on old standards and old ways of thinking. We cannot achieve the stellar results we expect in today's environment to follow or be following the old ways of doing things. We need to join the broken lines of our surroundings and get the business going in a different direction, break the line, and get busy.

The broken line may illustrate that the defensive or offensive positions are not solid or continuous along a particular stretch. This could be intentional, reflecting planned gaps or areas of limited defensive strength to allow for maneuverability or to draw an adversary into a specific location. What is your plan? Are there gaps? Who is your adversary?

The broken lines can be an issue when it comes to planning and providing leadership and employees with a visual representation of the operational concept, emphasizing flexibility and adaptability in the execution of organizational objectives and operations. Success comes from the ability to convey a nuanced understanding of the battles ahead and the intended movements or actions of the organization to pivot in the fast-paced world of business forces.

In this book, we will explore the world of startups, finance, and business education/information. Through a combination of practical advice and insightful anecdotes and examples, this book will take you on a journey to understand the intricacies of launching and growing a successful startup.

From securing funding to navigating the ever-changing and dynamic financial landscape that can be applied to today's startup organization. This book will provide insights and strategies for beginning a startup organization. Additionally, you will explore the importance of business education, mentorship, and advisors and how they can empower aspiring entrepreneurs.

This book is meant to create as many questions as answers. It is up to the reader to determine when and under what direction they should go. Every organization is on the hunt for money, and there are hundreds, if not thousands, of choices along the way. This book aims to stir the pot and get you thinking about what you truly want and how you can work toward your aspirations.

When funding anything, whether your home, business, land purchase or corporate acquisition, there are many issues and factors to consider. This book will explore and educate, inform, and liberate by talking about boring yet necessary topics. It was created to provide a few insights that will help you better your everyday life.

We are not looking to be the next great book on finance or funding, just a guide for those on the hunt and on the trial of cash and debt for their opportunity.

We do not claim to have all the answers; we don't have all the answers because most situations are independent and unique in the structure of the deal and the fiscal models used. What we are really attempting to do is give you our thoughts on many areas of finance, the pitfalls, the opportunities, and the experience that we have had in these areas.

We are not tax advisors or finance advisors. We are just a bunch of people who have had good and bad experiences in life and want to tell others what we have learned from them. You should always, with all your abilities and intelligence, do your own research and due diligence on every deal you propose and/or execute.

Foreword

It is with great pleasure and humility that I write this foreword for my friend, my brother, and my business partner, Christopher Schuring. Christopher has graciously afforded me the honor of providing this acknowledgment, and I am truly grateful.

As the old adage goes, *"You can't know where you're going unless you know where you've been."* This sentiment is at the core of why this book is such a fundamental primer on the principles of business success. Drawing on his 40 years of experience, the author has utilized his wealth of knowledge to provide an entrepreneurial roadmap for developing a thriving business model. He skillfully navigates the intricate balance of financial and operational strategies, equipping readers with the resources necessary to succeed in today's ever-evolving business landscape.

My own background lends credence to the importance of this work. As someone with a BA in political science from California State University Long Beach, I come from the non-profit public health sector, where I spent 40 years in executive management roles from San Francisco to Los Angeles. During this time, I was recognized as a policy expert, helping to shape state and national public policies for behavioral treatment services across the public health, criminal justice, and homeless sectors. In 2015, I began working with Atmospheric Water Generation technology, and in 2019, I was appointed as the CEO of Okavate Inc., leading the company toward a future where atmospheric water harvesting becomes a cornerstone of the new green economy. This journey has reinforced the significance of the principles outlined in this book, as they promote environmental justice, create new water markets with good-paying jobs, and bolster water security for both urban and rural communities.

In the wake of the COVID-19 pandemic, the financial and social landscape has undergone a profound transformation. This book provides invaluable leadership strategies, business acumen, and financing mechanisms that were not previously widely known or accessible to the general public. These tools have become essential in navigating the current global economy, which has shifted away from the US-centric structures of the past 40 years.

Christopher has meticulously researched and compiled this wealth of knowledge, drawing on the lessons learned through the trials and tribulations of his own professional career. It is with great humility and pleasure that I recommend this book to anyone seeking the keys to developing a successful business in the new, post-pandemic global economy. As someone who has been instrumental in my own journey through life, I can attest to the profound impact that Christopher's insights and guidance can have.

Gregory Senegal

CEO, Okavate Inc.

***

Mr. Senegal holds a BA in political science from California State University Long Beach and comes from the non-profit public health sector, where he spent 40 years in executive management from San Francisco to Los Angeles, such as Health Right 360 (SF) aka Walden House Inc and His Sheltering Arms (LA). Mr. Senegal is a recognized policy expert who helped develop state and national public policy for behavioral treatment services spanning the public health, criminal justice and homeless sectors.

In 2015, Gregory began working with an Atmospheric Water Generation organization. In 2019, Gregory was installed as the CEO of Okavate Inc. to lead the company in a direction where atmospheric water harvesting becomes a local point in the new green economy which promotes environmental justice, creates new water markets with good-paying jobs and bolsters water security for both urban and rural communities.

Prologue

I would like to tell you enough about me, the author, to give you a sense of who I am, as well as why you might find value in this book. It might even scare you a little bit, but that is part of the adventure. When we are a bit frightened, we seek solutions to our quandaries, and in that, we grow and gain wisdom, so here we go, hold on for the complete ride.

Here goes the personal introduction: my name is Christopher S Schuring, and I go by Chris unless I am in trouble, which is often. I will offer insight into my background, experiences, and motivations for writing this book, as well as others in the future. There may even be a few highlights and personal anecdotes that shaped my perspective. By the way, my perspective comes from all angles and places, from being a lumberjack to running international POPs, Point of Presence, around the globe, without a college education.

Let's begin the adventure with a bit of background as it relates to me, the author of this little diatribe hereinafter I will refer to Me or I, just so we are clear; it is all about me and what I have been up to for the past 63 years, as the author of this little adventure, experiences, failures (I believe they were all learning experiences) and conjectures as they relate to seeking investments, starting companies.

Let's begin the adventure with some background on my experiences, failures, and insights related to seeking investments, starting companies, and taking them to the next level.

I will introduce you, the reader, to a journey through my entrepreneurial path, laying the foundation for an in-depth exploration of the challenges and triumphs faced in the business world.

All of my experiences stem from the very beginning. I helped on the family paper route when I was around 8 to nine years old. From there, I started doing yard work, really anything, for money. I wanted a bike when I was 12; I needed to raise the money on my own, so I did just that: I worked hard, got the 72 dollars for the bike at the Military PX, and was off to the races. There was no stopping from there. It was the foundation for many, if not all, of work until the present day: work hard, make money, get the job done, take on the challenge, and get the reward. No one was going to do it for me.

I do not want to make this look like a resume, but I will touch on the highlights of my journey. I went from sweeping the neighbors' driveway to setting skeet at a gun range to raising hogs for profit in the 4-H organization, and then on to selling hogs to pay for an exchange trip to Japan when I was 15 and a half. It was a great time in Japan, on my own for the most part.

My real professional career started after I left the slaughterhouse where I worked to move to the San Jose Bay area in California. Prior to that move, I did things such as working as a furniture mover and installer, a cook, a dishwasher, a busboy, and a few other odd jobs. All of that taught me that you had to seek out opportunities and make your own way. Like most, if not all, startup founders.

These experiences created the initial spark that ignited my passion for entrepreneurship, the early stages of developing business ideas, and the practical steps taken to turn those ideas into reality. I will delve into the strategies I employed, the pivotal decisions made, and the relationships they built to grow their businesses in later sections, woven into the overall contents of the book, so pay attention. (By the way, paying attention is a key factor to success and finding opportunities.)

Don't let anyone tell you they have never failed; if that is true, they will not be a great teacher, in my humble opinion.

So, yes, I have "failures" that are significant because they acknowledge that the road to success I was on needed fixing, and it was less traveled and was often paved with setbacks. I place failures in quotes to indicate that they were education; it was my price to pay for not going to college. Remember, experience is a great teacher, but it does not have to be your experience; learning from others is less painful.

I can tell you about the time I was in the landscaping business, a company I called Blade Runner, and I went out of business due to competition and the fact that my crew was caught drinking on the job. Or the time I had a business partner in the digital graphics and labeling business called Total Media Access, and that partner took the bank account and disappeared; that was fun. The phone sales and installation company, called Best Choice Communications, and the top sales guy, my partner, and the guy with all the knowledge, got cancer. He later recovered, thank God, but that ended with a potential lawsuit from a client that cost the business, not much fun. One last one: in the energy business, I started a company called 2Cor9 in the solar field. We built the company fast; within 120 days, we had an offer to be purchased, so I took the deal, only to be scammed out of everything I owned, both professionally as well as personally, by what is called a Pump and Dump scheme.

All of this has placed a lot of wisdom in my way and along the journey. It is this wisdom that I want to share. I may not always be right, but hopefully, through experience, I can help you on your journey. By sharing these experiences, I not only highlight the resilience required in entrepreneurship but also offer valuable lessons learned from these experiences. These stories of failure can be just as enlightening, if not more so, than the success stories, as they provide real-world examples of the challenges entrepreneurs face and the importance of perseverance.

The insights come from the deeper understanding and wisdom that I have gained through my journey. These insights will include the nuances of securing investments, such as how to pitch effectively to investors, understanding what investors are looking for, and the importance of timing and networking. I will also share my perspective on what it takes to start a company—from ideation to execution—and the key factors that contribute to a business's ability to scale and reach the next level of growth. These insights are intended to provide readers with actionable advice and a clearer understanding of the complexities involved in entrepreneurship.

Overall, I want to set the stage for a comprehensive exploration of the author's entrepreneurial journey, providing readers with a blend of practical knowledge, personal anecdotes, and thoughtful reflections that can inspire and guide them on their own path to success.

I have a rich and diverse background in the world of entrepreneurship and startups, which entails being part of and leading capital raising and budget handling tasks. I have experienced the highs and lows of the entrepreneurial journey, gaining valuable insights along the way, with an extensive 50-year career in the technology and sales fields with advancement into executive management and business ownership. I have been involved in business ranging from Meat Processing to International data center management for the emerging dot com enterprises of the 1990s, as well as algae for carbon capture and storage, utility-grade solar design and installs, atmospheric water generation, waste to energy, and Smart City development, internationally. Why is this relevant? Through these experiences, a wealth of knowledge has been amassed and lived in the real world in real-world scenarios. This has been from success as well as failures and great learning experiences. While in the algae business, my partner and I completed a successful round of lobbying efforts in order to change the law to the tune of 1.5 billion dollars in favor of carbon capture and storage technologies.

Having achieved high-level management positions at several startup firms in strategic, tactical, sales, and marketing areas. Consulted and held TAB (Technical Advisory Board) and Board positions with several companies. Business ownership in the energy and energy consulting fields. I have experience in international business in Korea, Japan, the United Kingdom, Germany, China, India, Guatemala, and West Africa, as well as domestic operational development in New York, California.

As a Motivational speaker for sales organizations for five years, owning an internet-based radio station that had over 7,000 listeners a week being broadcast in 35 countries, having media interviews with NBC, CBS, CNBC, CNET, The Family Channel, Greta Wire, SMUD TV, newspapers, radio programs, host, and on-air personality. Conducted over 550 hours of talk time on various AM, FM, and Blog talk radio on the subject of solar and TEDx presentations. Hosted, engineered, produced, and conducted interviews for an online radio station that broadcasted to over 35 countries and had a listener base of several thousand listeners every week.

I have been a founder or partner in organizations from Landscaping to International Data Centers and POP operations.

And there are many other activities that have led to the formation of this text. Some of these will be dived into in the chapters that follow. (Oh and by the way I have also been a Lumberjack, Truck Driver OTR, Dish Washer, Cook, Body Guard, Set Skeet at a gun range, Warehouse Manager, USPS Letter Carrier, Printer Operator, Nuclear Power Plant Document Control Clerk, Courier Driver, Tree Trimmer, Landscaper, Painter, Roofer, Security Guard, Cobol Programmer, Database Analyst, Trained to be a Race Car Driver, and Radio Station Owner/Operator.) I have also been part of several startups and emerging organizations during what was called the Dot Com Boom and after in the energy industry.

It is with all of this that I felt it was time to sit down and gather my thoughts on the subject of startup funding, the process, and the issue as I see them. Now, I also understand that some will disagree with me on the point of context, and that is ok. If we can agree that there are options, and I may not know them, which I don't, then we can have a constructive conversation around strategy and relationships that lead to results.

For every notation and option that I write about, there are other options that lead to the same result; it is about being creative and being open to the possibility of options. A myopic approach in the marketplace will yield few results and additional frustration.

Let's get started, read on, and think as you go. Don't just read; imagine, dream, create passion, and expand the possibilities.

Contents

Chapter 1: What is Broken?

"If there is disturbance in the camp, the general's authority is weak."

-Sun Tzu, The Art of War

This quote reflects the idea that a system in disarray is often a sign of weak leadership or ineffective management, indicating fundamental flaws in its structure or operation.

What is Broken – It's not a question but a description

In this chapter, I will address the common challenges and highlight where I believe the system is flawed. Every business owner must grasp both sides of these issues. Without this understanding, how can one adopt an innovative approach without "*burning all the boats*"? It's fine to watch the boats burn from the shore, but remember, you're not alone—your team is with you, and they care as much about your success as you do. Don't burn them along the way.

Many startups have flawed financial strategies, often driven by overly optimistic projections, poor financial planning, and mismatched funding strategies. While this view may seem harsh, it can be corrected. Often, startups seek advice from well-meaning but inexperienced people, typically within the "*friends and family*" circle, who haven't been in their position.

Founders tend to overestimate revenue growth and underestimate expenses, leading to a high burn rate that exceeds their financial runway. This flawed approach arises from several key factors I'll discuss. It becomes problematic when driven by the desire for funding that's not aligned with the organization's needs. In new organizations, projections are often inconsistent, and external pressures to inflate numbers can cause investors to lose trust and derail expectations. Here are some points to ponder:

Overly Optimistic Projections: Startups often base financial projections on ideal scenarios, expecting rapid user adoption and exponential revenue growth. This excessive optimism can result in unrealistic revenue targets and a failure to anticipate market challenges or competition.

When this occurs, it can mislead investors about the true opportunity. This breakdown puts unnecessary pressure on the organization. The solution is to be honest with yourself, your team, and your investors. Clearly outline all risks and how your team plans to address them. Once you've set your projections, scale them back by 15% and explain that while issues may arise, your team is prepared to recoup the difference. The point is to be realistic—set slightly optimistic projections, then present a scaled-back version to demonstrate you're grounded in reality, not simply following advice. Projections are just estimates; as long as they're balanced with reality and scalability, you'll be fine. It's better to exceed expectations than to fall short.

Inadequate Financial Planning: Many startups lack thorough financial planning, often underestimating critical expenses like marketing, staffing, product development, and unforeseen contingencies. This oversight can significantly strain resources.

Financial planning often gets muddled between personal and business finances, but we'll focus on the business side here. A solid financial plan typically spans five years or more, aligning projections with expenses. One commonly overlooked aspect is the balance between cash burn and cash earned. Effective planning should include strategies for leveraging cash on hand to increase value. For example, if you have $500,000 unused for 60 days, how can you grow it without risk? Proper cash management might involve using sweep accounts to earn weekly interest or partnering with individuals who can help leverage cash through fractional banking processes. These strategies should be integral to your financial plan and cash management objectives.

Misaligned Funding Strategies: One of the most critical missteps startups can make is pursuing funding strategies that don't align with their business model or growth stage. For instance, securing a large amount of venture capital too early can create immense pressure to scale at a pace that may not be sustainable. Conversely, seeking too little funding can leave startups undercapitalized, preventing them from reaching key milestones or adapting to market changes effectively.

The strategy you adopt for funding directly influences both the short-term and long-term trajectory of your business. It's essential to look beyond immediate goals and think about where you want the company to be in the future. Every funding decision should consider the "*end zone*" rather than just the "*goal line.*" By focusing on long-term sustainability, you avoid the risk of over-funding or under-funding, both of which can harm your startup.

A well-thought-out strategy involves scaling investments based on performance—both internal and external. This scaling ensures that you're funded appropriately and don't dilute equity prematurely, which can erode the ownership stake of early founders and investors. For example, a structured equity plan can minimize the dilution of stock holdings while maximizing your ability to secure necessary resources.

Additionally, founders should explore diverse funding strategies. This can include alternative income sources like earning commissions or consulting fees through partnerships or referrals in unrelated fields, such as real estate. While your core focus should always be on your startup, don't overlook opportunities that could help you bring in capital with minimal effort. Partnering with others for specific transactions or deals can allow you to generate working capital without deviating from your primary business focus. Keeping an open mind to such opportunities can enhance your liquidity and give you the financial flexibility to invest in your company's growth.

Chronic Burn Rate: Another major issue facing startups is a chronic burn rate—where the company spends more money than it generates. This can quickly deplete the startup's financial runway, forcing founders into urgent, often less favorable fundraising situations or making them resort to drastic cost-cutting measures.

A high burn rate is typically driven by a combination of overly optimistic revenue forecasts and underestimated expenses. However, it's not just direct costs like product development or salaries that contribute to this issue. Founders often forget to account for various other expenses that can quietly chip away at their finances. These include taxes, employment-related costs (such as payroll taxes and benefits), lease payments, utilities, and online services critical to maintaining the company's digital presence.

Employee benefits, in particular, can dramatically increase your burn rate. In some cases, benefits can account for up to 75% of base salaries, especially when healthcare and retirement contributions are factored in. Founders need to be aware of all these expenses and account for them in their financial planning.

When it comes to managing burn rate, honesty is crucial—both with yourself and with your team. If the situation calls for slowing down growth to preserve cash, that may be a better option than running out of money prematurely and having to close your doors. One strategy to manage the burn rate effectively is outsourcing tasks that fall outside your core expertise. If HR, for example, is not a core competency, outsource it. You can pay a set fee to have experts manage those functions, freeing you to focus on the areas where you and your team excel—such as innovation, product development, and growth.

Lack of Financial Expertise: Many founders, particularly those from technical or non-financial backgrounds, lack the expertise to develop strong financial strategies. This gap can lead to poor decision-making, reliance on inaccurate financial models, and an overall lack of financial accountability.

Finance can be daunting, even for experts. As a founder, you're juggling many responsibilities—focusing on the business, building your product, leading your team, and more. It's understandable that financial management may not be your top priority. However, neglecting this area can have significant consequences for the health and growth of your startup.

One way to address this is by seeking assistance from outside financial experts. These professionals can provide valuable insight into your business's financial health and offer an unbiased perspective on areas that may need improvement. They can also guide you in navigating the complexities of tax issues, compliance, and non-traditional financing methods, such as fractional banking.

However, even with expert help, it's important to stay engaged in the financial process. Ultimately, you are responsible for the financial decisions made in your startup. By understanding the financial landscape, you can make informed choices that benefit the long-term sustainability of your company.

To mitigate these financial risks, it's essential for startups to adopt a more conservative approach to financial projections. Instead of assuming best-case scenarios, founders should account for potential challenges, such as market fluctuations, unforeseen costs, or delays in reaching revenue milestones. A realistic, cautious projection allows for greater flexibility and helps avoid situations where the company needs to make desperate funding or cost-cutting decisions.

Comprehensive financial planning is another critical element. Startups should have a detailed financial plan that accounts for all potential costs and revenue streams. This plan should be flexible enough to adjust for any changes in the business environment. Additionally, aligning your funding strategy with realistic business goals can help ensure that you don't take on more capital than needed, nor do you leave yourself undercapitalized.

Diversifying funding sources can also protect against financial vulnerability. While venture capital is a common source of funding for startups, relying too heavily on it can leave you exposed to market downturns or shifts in investor sentiment. Explore other funding avenues, such as government grants, angel investors, and revenue-based financing, to build a more stable financial foundation.

Finally, maintaining rigorous financial controls and accountability is crucial for managing cash flow effectively. Regular audits, real-time cash flow tracking, and clear financial reporting processes will help you spot problems early and address them before they spiral out of control.

Top Indicators of Financial Misalignment:

By adopting a measured, diversified approach to funding, controlling burn rate, and seeking financial expertise, startups can set themselves up for sustainable growth while minimizing financial risks.

Identifying the top indicators of poor financial controls and over-reliance on venture capital in startups can help diagnose potential problems early. Here are ten key indicators:

1. **High Burn Rate**: The startup is spending more money than it is generating in revenue, depleting its cash reserves quickly.
2. **Lack of Budgeting and Forecasting**: The absence of detailed financial plans and projections leads to an inability to anticipate cash flow needs and manage expenses.
3. **Inconsistent Financial Reporting**: Irregular or inaccurate financial statements make it difficult to track the financial health of the business.
4. **Dependence on a Single Funding Source**: Reliance primarily on venture capital without exploring other funding options like debt financing, grants, or revenue-based financing.
5. **Frequent Capital Raising**: The need to constantly raise new rounds of funding to stay afloat indicates an unsustainable business model.
6. **Poor Cash Flow Management**: Inability to manage the timing of cash inflows and outflows, leading to periods of severe cash shortages.
7. **Weak Internal Controls**: Lack of robust processes for expense approvals, financial reconciliations, and fraud prevention.
8. **Investor Pressure and Influence**: Investors have a heavy influence on company decisions, often leading

to a focus on short-term growth metrics rather than long-term sustainability.

9. **Inadequate Reserves**: Insufficient cash reserves to handle unexpected expenses or downturns in the market.

10. **High Operational Costs**: Excessive spending on non-essential areas like lavish offices, perks, and marketing without a clear return on investment.

Addressing Financial Misalignment and Diversifying Startup Growth Strategies

Addressing the financial misalignment that plagues many startups involves the implementation of stricter financial controls, diversifying funding sources, and adopting a more sustainable approach to growth and expenditure. Startups often feel the relentless pressure to scale rapidly within the ecosystem, with a disproportionate emphasis on growth over profitability. This is fueled by the pursuit of market share, attracting significant investments, and outpacing competitors. However, while the allure of swift expansion is understandable, it can come at the expense of building a sustainable business model.

Startups may engage in aggressive marketing, steep discounting, or over-hiring to drive growth. These tactics are often used without ensuring that the foundation of the business is sound in terms of revenue generation and operational efficiency. As a result, companies find themselves in a fragile financial situation, where they are continuously dependent on external funding to sustain day-to-day operations. When a company scales too quickly without the right financial controls or infrastructure, any disruption—whether from market shifts, loss of investor confidence, or internal mismanagement—can trigger a cash flow crisis.

At the core of this problem is the disconnect between scaling and profitability. Startups must recognize that growth alone is not a reliable indicator of long-term success. Without a clear path to profitability, companies are at risk of being unable to cover their operational costs, leading to mounting debts and growing investor dissatisfaction. If a company's burn rate exceeds its revenue and the runway runs out, the startup may face premature failure. This highlights the importance of balancing the drive for rapid scaling with financial sustainability to ensure lasting success.

The Broken Funding Ecosystem: A Double-Edged Sword

The current state of startup funding is often described as broken. Several interconnected issues hinder its effectiveness and threaten to derail the long-term potential of the ecosystem. One of the primary problems is the overwhelming focus on startups with high-growth potential and the capacity for rapid scalability. Venture capital firms and investors are drawn to these companies because of their potential for quick returns, but this approach forces startups into a high-stakes race to expand rapidly.

This emphasis on rapid growth can have detrimental effects. Startups are pushed to scale prematurely before they have adequately fine-tuned their operations or achieved product-market fit. As a result, many companies face operational missteps, unsustainable expenses, and financial instability. In this environment, startups are pressured to show short-term results at the expense of long-term stability, leaving even promising ventures vulnerable to failure.

Another issue is the concentration of funding in specific geographic regions and sectors. The tech hubs of Silicon Valley, New York, and a few other cities dominate venture capital allocations, leaving startups in other regions struggling to secure resources. This geographical bias means that many innovative ideas emerging outside these hotspots go unnoticed and unfunded, limiting diversity in the entrepreneurial landscape. The concentration of funding in sectors like tech and software further narrows the focus, ignoring potential breakthroughs in fields such as clean energy, healthcare, or manufacturing.

This geographical and sector-based bias is compounded by the reliance on personal networks for fundraising. Founders who lack access to the exclusive circles of venture capital and angel investors are often at a significant disadvantage, particularly those from underrepresented backgrounds. Underrepresented founders face additional challenges, including biases in the funding process and fewer opportunities to pitch their businesses to influential investors. This dynamic exacerbates the inequalities in the entrepreneurial ecosystem, further marginalizing those who already face significant barriers.

The Unicorn Culture: Uneven Resource Allocation

The intense competition for funding creates a “unicorn” culture, where only a small number of standout companies receive the lion’s share of investment. These companies—those valued at over $1 billion—are often seen as the holy grail of the startup ecosystem, capturing the imagination of both the media and investors. However, this disproportionate focus on a few high-profile companies means that many viable businesses struggle to attract support despite having strong potential for innovation and growth.

The overemphasis on a handful of unicorns skews the startup ecosystem toward a narrow set of industries and business models. While the companies that receive significant funding often show rapid growth and scalability, many other promising sectors are left underfunded. This stifles innovation across industries such as biotech, sustainability, and education, where progress often requires more patient capital and longer development timelines. By prioritizing quick profits and scalable models over sustainability and diversity, the current funding landscape fails to nurture a broad-based, inclusive startup culture.

Building a More Inclusive and Sustainable Startup Ecosystem

The issues described above underscore the urgent need to rethink how startups are funded. Instead of prioritizing rapid growth and quick returns, there should be a greater emphasis on building sustainable, long-term business models. This means encouraging startups to focus on creating products and services that solve real problems while ensuring that their financial structure can support growth over the long term.

Startups can take several steps to achieve this. First, they must implement rigorous financial controls, ensuring that growth is managed in a way that aligns with cash flow and operational capabilities. Startups should also diversify their funding sources, seeking out alternative forms of financing, such as revenue-based financing, government grants, or strategic partnerships, to reduce their reliance on venture capital.

In addition, investors and venture capital firms must play a role in fostering a more inclusive and sustainable ecosystem. This includes expanding their geographic and sectoral focus to include underrepresented founders and regions and investing in companies with longer-term growth potential, even if they may not show immediate results. By addressing these issues, the startup ecosystem can become more equitable, resilient, and capable of driving innovation across a broader range of industries and regions.

In conclusion, startups must strike a balance between rapid scaling and financial sustainability. By focusing on sustainable business practices and diversifying funding, both startups and investors can work together to build a more dynamic, inclusive, and successful entrepreneurial landscape.

Chapter 2: Why Is It Broken – No Blame It Just Is

"If you know the enemy and know yourself, you need not fear the result of a hundred battles."

-Sun Tzu

The standard set of issues may outline where you feel something is broken, but that is just a starting point. To truly understand the "big why" behind the issues, you need to define them in the context of your specific business and goals. This guide is meant to help you identify what is broken and why, but the real work is to relate those problems back to your unique situation and objectives.

Every business owner needs to consider multiple perspectives on an issue. If they don't fully grasp the problem from different angles, how can they resolve it and run a successful operation? Sometimes, an outside resource, like this guide, can help clear the path to deeper understanding. Let's push aside some of the obstacles obscuring the way forward.

Comprehending both sides of the issue is crucial to understanding why the overall system, and potentially your own systems, are broken. Don't dwell on regrets or major concerns - once we identify what is broken and why, we can work to fix it or pivot in a better direction.

A thriving business is built on accurate, actionable information. Approach all of this as data to improve your understanding and develop greater wisdom.

1. Common Issues in Business Operations

This is one of my greatest areas of development, operational strategy, and oversight. I started in the computer world at Atari as an operations analyst over the corporation's financial systems—the computer side, not the accounting side.

Every business, whether a fledgling startup or a well-established company, grapples with a set of fundamental challenges that can profoundly impact its capacity to operate efficiently and expand. Let's explore these challenges in greater depth to comprehend their implications better.

Financial Management

Effective financial management is the cornerstone of any successful business. It involves meticulously tracking day-to-day expenses and making strategic long-term economic decisions to sustain the organization. However, many companies grapple with cash flow management—ensuring there is always sufficient capital on hand to fulfill obligations like payroll, rent, and supplier payments.

This challenge is particularly acute for small businesses, which may lack access to substantial reserves or lines of credit. Budgeting is another critical aspect, where companies must carefully allocate resources to various departments while ensuring they don't overspend. Financial forecasting, the process of predicting future revenues, expenses, and profits, is essential for planning and informed decision-making. Nonetheless, inaccurate forecasts can lead to poor choices, such as overexpansion, underfunding crucial projects, or misallocating resources, which can severely hamper growth and stability.

Human Resources

The success of any business largely depends on its people, making human resource management a critical function. Hiring the right talent is often challenging, especially in competitive industries where skilled workers are in high demand. Once hired, retaining these valuable employees becomes another significant hurdle. High turnover can be costly, not only in terms of the direct expenses associated with recruiting and training new staff but also due to the loss of institutional knowledge and the disruption it causes within teams.

Training and development are crucial for keeping employees motivated and ensuring they possess the necessary skills to contribute effectively to the business. Moreover, managing employee relations—guaranteeing that staff are engaged, satisfied, and aligned with the company's goals—is essential. When human resource issues are not adequately addressed, they can lead to a toxic work environment, decreased productivity, and, ultimately, a negative impact on the business's bottom line.

Operational Efficiency

Operational efficiency refers to how effectively a business converts resources (such as labor, materials, and technology) into goods and services. Inefficiencies in operations can arise from various factors, including outdated processes, poor workflow management, and ineffective use of technology. For instance, a manufacturing company might struggle with production bottlenecks due to outdated machinery, or a service-based business might experience delays because of inefficient scheduling systems. Supply chain management is another area where inefficiencies can cause significant disruptions, such as delayed deliveries, increased costs, and inventory shortages.

Operational inefficiencies increase costs and can result in poor customer experiences, such as late deliveries or inconsistent product quality. Businesses that fail to address these inefficiencies risk falling behind competitors who can deliver the same products or services faster and at a lower cost.

Customer Satisfaction

Customer satisfaction is not just about meeting expectations but exceeding them consistently. However, achieving this balance is often challenging. Business owners must understand their customers' needs and preferences and tailor their offerings accordingly. For example, a restaurant must not only serve good food but also ensure a pleasant dining experience, which includes factors like ambiance, service, and cleanliness. However, in trying to please customers, businesses might overcommit—offering faster delivery times than they can manage or promising features that are not feasible.

This can lead to dissatisfaction when the business fails to deliver on its promises. On the other hand, underestimating what customers want can lead to a lack of innovation and missed growth opportunities. For instance, a tech company that fails to update its software in line with user feedback may lose customers to competitors offering more user-friendly alternatives. Consistently meeting and exceeding customer expectations is crucial for building loyalty and fostering long-term relationships, which are key to sustained success.

Compliance and Legal Issues

Compliance with legal and regulatory requirements is a non-negotiable aspect of running a business. However, the complexity and ever-evolving nature of regulations makes this a daunting task. Businesses must navigate various laws, including those related to taxes, labor, environmental impact, and industry-specific regulations. For example, a small business might struggle to keep up with changes in tax laws, leading to filing errors and potential penalties.

In highly regulated industries like healthcare or finance, the stakes are even higher, with strict requirements around data privacy, reporting, and consumer protection. Non-compliance can result in severe consequences, including fines, legal action, and significant damage to the company's reputation. Beyond just avoiding penalties, proactive compliance is also an opportunity for businesses to build trust with customers and stakeholders by demonstrating their commitment to ethical practices and legal obligations.

2. Where the System is Broken

Understanding the common challenges is crucial, but many businesses fail to address these issues effectively. The system often breaks down here, leading to persistent problems and missed opportunities.

Lack of Awareness

As we further explore the specific issues, it is critical to maintain comprehensive awareness of everything within your business and your financial strategies. I was recently working with a team that was thriving in the technology arena, efficiently collecting and compiling data points. They utilized these data points to run the software solutions they had developed, but they had overlooked a crucial aspect: the data collection process itself.

After a few consultations, they realized the data was as valuable, if not more so, than the software. By detailing the data collection process, they were able to leverage it in the area of finance, as they now had another valued product to offer their clients - a service they had not previously considered.

A lack of awareness is one of the most significant barriers to addressing these challenges. Many business owners are so focused on day-to-day operations that they overlook the underlying issues that can lead to bigger problems down the line.

For instance, a small business owner might be so busy trying to keep the business running that they don't notice the signs of financial trouble, such as consistently low cash reserves or growing debt. This lack of awareness can also extend to external factors, such as changes in market conditions, new regulations, or shifts in customer preferences. Without a clear understanding of these issues, business owners are ill-equipped to respond effectively, leading to a reactive rather than proactive approach to problem-solving.

When it comes to finance, it is even more critical to understand and research fiscal strategies and opportunities, such as:

- Commissions from outside sales that can be used in your bottom line for operational purposes
- Referring others to finance and product assistance to leverage your relationships
- Understand fractional banking and the opportunities it provides
- Purchase order, PO, financing
- Hard money loans for you and others (you can gain a commission for referrals)
- External finance transactions that require little to no effort and can yield great results
- Affiliate programs that can generate repetitive cash flow with little to no work

We will get into more details later on all of these, which can ease the burden of finance. You should be aware of them and understand their core workings.

Inadequate Solutions

Even when problems are recognized, the solutions often fall short. This could be due to a lack of resources, such as time, money, or expertise, or it could stem from a superficial understanding of the problem. For example, a business might recognize that its customer satisfaction levels are dropping and respond by offering discounts or promotions. While this might provide a short-term boost, it doesn't address the root cause of the dissatisfaction, such as poor product quality or inadequate customer service. Another example could be a company that identifies a bottleneck in its production process and decides to invest in new equipment. However, if the issue lies with the workflow or employee training, the new equipment may not solve the problem and could even exacerbate it by adding complexity. Inadequate solutions often result in wasted resources and missed opportunities for meaningful improvement.

Solutions are best generated through a collaborative *"think tank"* approach, where a joint effort is applied. Many times, we try to develop solutions on our own, perhaps feeling compelled not to involve others to avoid revealing any secrets. However, we need to come together as a team to find the most effective solutions. It may also take an outside entity or a team member from another part of the company to provide a fresh perspective.

I often find my most valuable solutions through business networking and discussions with others about the challenges they are facing rather than solely focusing on my own problems.

Help others, and solutions will find you. Oh, by the way, not all solutions will work; that is where wisdom is created. Have fun with that. Embrace the process and have fun with it.

As an example, our solar company investigated feed-in tariffs as a way to conduct business. Our competition was building large ground-mount arrays, which seemed like a good approach. However, after we came together as a team and closely reviewed the regulations and policies, we found that most people only knew what others had told them and had never even read the manuals themselves. By taking the time to truly understand the details, we discovered a better way forward and selected an approach that enabled us to gain sales and funding. We utilized the same methods as cellular tower leasing for smaller, more manageable arrays on private property, and it proved to be a great success.

Similarly, our algae company was initially designed to provide carbon capture and storage solutions for the energy industry. Our starting point was a potential biofuel company focused on the cultivation of the jatropha plant. But after conducting thorough research, meeting with experts, and collaborating as a team, we decided the crop opportunity was not viable. Then, at a biofuel conference, the President of an oil company mentioned they would invest 500 million dollars in algae. We seized the opportunity to pivot right then and there. By being open-minded and willing to explore new directions, we were able to raise money for the algae project and establish a thriving business.

Resistance to Change

Change is a constant in business, but it's also something that many organizations stubbornly resist. This resistance can stem from a variety of factors, including fear of the unknown, comfort with the status quo, or a lack of understanding of the benefits that change can bring. For example, a business that has been successful for many years might resist adopting new technologies or processes, believing that "if it's not broken, don't fix it." However, this mindset can lead to stagnation, as competitors who are more willing to innovate and adapt to changing market conditions pull ahead. Resistance to change can also be driven by employees who are comfortable with the current way of doing things and fear that new processes or technologies will disrupt their routines or threaten their jobs. Overcoming this resistance requires strong leadership, clear communication, and a willingness to invest in training and support.

As with our algae business and others, we recognized the need to change, and we did just that. In some of the positions I've held over my career, I was tasked with evaluating operational policies and personnel. In those evaluations, I was sometimes required to remove staff due to their resistance to change. The key is not to resist but rather to educate, research, pivot, and regroup in all areas, not just finance.

In finance, the change has already taken place; the mainstream just has not informed you. The old ways of getting funded via venture capital and private equity firms are vastly different from what they have been telling you; we will go into more detail later.

Poor Communication

Communication is a critical component of any business operation, but it's an area where many organizations often struggle. Poor communication can lead to misunderstandings, misaligned goals, and ineffective execution of strategies. For instance, if a company's leadership team decides to implement a new strategy but fails to clearly communicate the reasons behind the change and how it will benefit the organization, employees may be resistant or disengaged, leading to poor implementation.

Similarly, if frontline employees are not kept informed about changes in customer preferences or new company policies, they may continue operating as usual, leading to missed opportunities or even customer dissatisfaction. In another example, departments within a company may operate in silos, with little communication or collaboration between them, resulting in inefficiencies as teams duplicate efforts or fail to leverage each other's expertise.

Effective communication requires clear, consistent messaging from leadership, as well as channels for feedback and collaboration across all levels of the organization. Success is ultimately built on effective communication. While communication is not always easy, it is a critical skill to develop. Maintain a calm, thoughtful approach, as business can be personal and filled with emotion. Do not let these emotions control you or your team. Communication should never be discounted and always be clear and honest, especially in finance, where it should be documented in writing and fully understood by all parties.

3. The Importance of Understanding

Given the complex nature of these challenges and the potential pitfalls in addressing them, it's clear that a deep understanding is essential for any business owner. Without this understanding, efforts to improve operations and finance are likely to be haphazard and ineffective.

Effective Decision-Making

Informed decisions are the foundation of successful business operations. When business owners have a comprehensive understanding of their challenges, they are better equipped to make decisions that will lead to positive outcomes. For example, a business owner who thoroughly comprehends their company's financial situation will be more likely to make prudent decisions about budgeting, investments, and cost-cutting measures.

Similarly, a leader who recognizes the importance of employee satisfaction and retention will invest in training, development, and workplace culture, leading to a more motivated and productive workforce. Effective decision-making also involves understanding the potential consequences of different actions and carefully weighing the risks and benefits before proceeding. This strategic approach helps businesses avoid common pitfalls and seize opportunities for growth and improvement.

The emphasis is on the word **informed**. Whenever possible, do your research; I do research even if I am not responsible directly. That way, in meetings and conversations, I can have a working knowledge of the topic so as not to be swayed in the wrong direction. As a founder and/or executive, you are the one who needs to make the decisions. A failure of many organizations is when the leaders fail to make a desired decision and take action around that decision. Also, not all decisions will be the right ones, but a decision needs to be made.

Operational Success

Understanding the common challenges and identifying where the system is broken are crucial first steps toward achieving operational success. When business owners can identify and address the root causes of inefficiencies, poor performance, and customer dissatisfaction, they can streamline operations and improve overall performance.

For instance, by recognizing that poor customer satisfaction is linked to inconsistent product quality, a business can focus on improving its production processes, leading to higher customer satisfaction and repeat business. Similarly, by addressing bottlenecks in the supply chain, a company can reduce delays and lower costs, resulting in more efficient operations and better margins. Operational success is not just about fixing problems as they arise but about creating a culture of continuous improvement, where issues are identified and addressed before they become critical.

Finance is a fundamental function of operations; without it, operations cease to function, and your business grinds to a halt. You need to evaluate your finances just as thoroughly as you do all other parts of your business. If you are weak in fiscal strategies, then consider hiring a team or individual who is strong in that area. Unfortunately, many companies have a broken fiscal strategy; they simply run every day like the last without adapting to the changing world around them. You need to be one step ahead, not just of your competition, but of the evolving market landscape.

The fiscal strategies that were taught, perhaps when you went to school, are often outdated and non-functional. It is critical that you take the time to conduct thorough research and become an expert in the field. This will prove to be a great way to outpace your competitors and achieve long-term success.

Sustained Growth and Competitiveness

In a competitive market, businesses that fail to understand and address their challenges will likely fall behind. On the other hand, those who take the time to understand both the common challenges and the specific issues within their operations are better positioned to adapt, innovate, and grow. For example, a business that stays on top of regulatory changes and proactively adjusts its operations to remain compliant can avoid costly fines and maintain a positive reputation with customers and stakeholders.

Similarly, a company that invests in understanding customer needs and trends can innovate faster and bring new products or services to market more quickly than its competitors. Sustained growth and competitiveness require a proactive approach to problem-solving, where business owners are constantly seeking to understand their environment, anticipate changes, and adapt their strategies accordingly.

To operate a successful business, it’s not enough to recognize the standard set of challenges that all businesses face. Owners must delve deeper, understanding the root causes of these challenges and where their systems may be falling short. This comprehensive understanding is the key to making informed decisions, improving operations, and achieving long-term success. Without it, businesses are likely to find themselves in a cycle of reacting to problems rather than proactively addressing them, ultimately limiting their potential for growth and success.

Chapter 3: Passion

Engage people with what they expect; it is what they are able to discern and confirms their projections. It settles them into predictable patterns of response, occupying their minds while you wait for the extraordinary moment — that which they cannot anticipate.

Passion can be a powerful motivator and a driving force behind the decision to start a business. While it's not an absolute requirement for every entrepreneur, it often plays a significant role in the success and longevity of a startup or any organization striving to make a meaningful impact in the world.

This passion fuels the energy and commitment needed to turn an idea into reality, especially during the challenging and uncertain early stages. When entrepreneurs are passionate about their vision, they are more likely to persevere through obstacles, adapt to changes, and stay focused on their long-term goals. This passion often translates into a deep sense of purpose, which not only inspires the founders but also attracts like-minded individuals—whether employees, customers, or investors—who share the same enthusiasm for the mission.

Companies driven by a clear and passionate vision tend to be more resilient, innovative, and capable of making a lasting impact, particularly for organizations aiming to create meaningful change in the world. Passion helps maintain momentum, even when faced with setbacks or market fluctuations.

For mission-driven organizations, passion is likely a cornerstone of their strategy, as it drives their efforts to solve problems, create value, and inspire others to join the journey. This passion not only helps achieve business objectives but also builds a legacy that extends beyond financial success, creating a positive and lasting influence on the communities and industries they serve. The role of passion in overcoming challenges, inspiring others, and achieving long-term success cannot be overstated, especially for organizations committed to making a significant impact.

Passion plays a crucial role in the world of entrepreneurship. When individuals are deeply passionate about a particular idea, cause, or industry, that passion can serve as a powerful motivator that drives them to start and build a successful company. Here are several ways in which passion contributes to the entrepreneurial journey:

Passion Fuels Persistence:

Starting and growing a business often involves facing numerous challenges and setbacks. However, a deep passion for the mission or product can provide the resilience needed to overcome obstacles and keep going, even in the face of adversity. The intrinsic joy and fulfillment that come from pursuing something you're passionate about can be a sustaining factor during times of difficulty.

Passion as a Driving Force:

When you're passionate about something, whether it's a personal goal, a project, or a cause, that passion serves as a powerful motivator. It gives you the energy, enthusiasm, and determination needed to overcome obstacles and keep pushing forward, even when faced with challenges. This passion acts as a driving force that fuels your commitment and helps you stay focused on your objectives.

Passion and Creative Thinking:

Passionate entrepreneurs are more likely to think creatively and seek innovative solutions to problems. They are driven to find better ways of doing things and are more inclined to push boundaries and take risks to bring their vision to life. Creative thinking and innovation often involve approaching problems from new perspectives and finding unique solutions.

In essence, passion becomes a source of resilience, transforming setbacks into learning experiences and fueling the determination needed to persevere in the face of adversity. The combination of passion and persistence is a potent formula for achieving long-term success and personal fulfillment as an entrepreneur.

Here are some general strategies to stimulate creative thinking and foster innovation:

Mind Mapping: Create a visual representation of ideas using mind maps. This can help you see connections between different elements and spark new insights.

Brainstorming: Encourage open and free-flowing idea generation. Avoid judgment and criticism during the initial phase to allow for a wide range of ideas.

Reverse Thinking: Consider the problem from the opposite perspective. What if you were trying to cause the problem? This can lead to unconventional solutions.

Cross-disciplinary Collaboration: Work with individuals from diverse backgrounds and fields. Different perspectives can bring in unique insights and approaches.

Analogies and Metaphors: Draw parallels between your problem and unrelated concepts. Metaphors can provide fresh perspectives and lead to innovative solutions.

rototyping and Iteration: Build small-scale prototypes to test and refine your ideas. Iterative processes often lead to improvements and unexpected breakthroughs.

Observation and Empathy: Understand the problem by observing people and empathizing with their experiences. This can lead to solutions that address real needs.

Challenge Assumptions: Question the assumptions underlying the problem. Sometimes, the most innovative solutions come from challenging the status quo.

Random Stimuli: Introduce random elements or stimuli to your thinking process. This could be as simple as choosing a random word and trying to connect it to your problem.

Technology Integration: Explore how emerging technologies can be applied to solve your problem. Technologies like AI, blockchain, or augmented reality may offer new possibilities.

Crowdsourcing Ideas: Seek input from a diverse group of people to gather a wide range of ideas. Online platforms and communities can be valuable resources.

Environmental Change: Sometimes, a change in the environment or surroundings can trigger fresh ideas. Consider working in a different location or exposing yourself to new stimuli.

Remember that creativity and innovation are iterative processes. It's okay to experiment, fail, and learn from experience. Embrace a mindset that welcomes curiosity, exploration, and the willingness to challenge conventional thinking.

Fostering creativity is a continuous process. By integrating the various approaches we discussed into your problem-solving strategies, you can create an environment where innovative solutions are more likely to emerge, driven by the passion of the team.

Passion is contagious. When entrepreneurs are truly passionate about their work, they inspire and motivate others, including team members, investors, and customers. This can create a positive and dynamic environment that fosters collaboration and success.

Entrepreneurs who are passionate about their work are more likely to stay focused and committed to their goals. Their sense of purpose and direction helps them prioritize tasks and make decisions aligned with the company's overall mission. They are also more likely to bounce back from failures and setbacks, navigating challenges with a positive mindset and learning from their experiences.

Passion often translates into a deep understanding of customers' needs and desires. Entrepreneurs passionate about their products or services are better equipped to connect with their target audience and create offerings that resonate.

They are also more likely to have a long-term vision for their company, driven by a desire to make a lasting impact and contribute something meaningful. While passion is a powerful motivator, successful entrepreneurship also requires strategic planning, adaptability, and effective execution.

Entrepreneurship can be challenging and demanding, especially in the early stages. Passion provides the resilience and determination needed to persevere through tough times. This intrinsic motivation, deeply connected to one's values, interests, and personal goals, sustains effort over the long term, which is crucial for overcoming obstacles and weathering difficult circumstances.

Passion tends to **foster a positive mindset**. When individuals genuinely love what they're doing or working toward, it becomes easier to perceive setbacks as learning opportunities rather than insurmountable obstacles. This positive outlook is a key component of resilience.

Passion often involves a strong **desire to achieve** or experience something. This drive can make entrepreneurs more adaptable in the face of challenges, as they may be more willing to adjust their approach, learn new skills, or seek alternative solutions to overcome obstacles.

Passion **provides emotional endurance**. It gives individuals the strength to persevere through difficult times, navigate uncertainties, and cope with failures. This emotional resilience is crucial for maintaining focus and determination.

Passion brings **clarity to goals and aspirations**. When one is clear about their objectives, it becomes easier to stay on course, even when the journey is tough. This sense of purpose contributes to perseverance.

Pursuing one's passion often brings a **sense of fulfillment** and satisfaction. This intrinsic reward system reinforces the commitment to the journey, making it easier to endure challenges for the sake of something truly cared about.

In summary, passion **acts as a driving force** that sustains motivation, fosters resilience, and provides the determination needed to persevere through tough times. It is a valuable asset that can help individuals overcome obstacles and achieve their long-term goals.

Enthusiastic employees are more likely to provide excellent customer service. When customers interact with positive and passionate individuals, it can enhance their overall experience, leading to repeat business and advocacy.

Both leaders and team members should recognize the impact of enthusiasm on the work environment and actively cultivate a positive and enthusiastic atmosphere. Encouraging open communication, celebrating achievements, and fostering a culture of appreciation can contribute to sustaining enthusiasm in the workplace.

Passion for a product or service can translate into a deep understanding of customer needs and a genuine desire to solve their problems. This customer-centric approach can lead to better product-market fit.

This enthusiasm can make one a more engaging and persuasive communicator when seeking investors, partners, or customers. It can help convey the significance and potential of a startup.

While passion can provide the emotional fuel and determination needed to start and grow a company, it should be complemented by a solid foundation of business skills, market knowledge, and effective execution. Combining passion with practicality is often the key to entrepreneurial success.

However, although it's a driving force, it's important to recognize that passion alone will not sustain a business through hardships. It is up to you, as the leader, to channel that passion in a way that motivates and guides your team.

When I entered the water solutions industry, I initially saw it as just another business opportunity with potential for financial gain. However, as I delved deeper into the industry and understood the critical importance of water as a fundamental element of life, my passion started to grow. Talking to others who shared this passion helped me further cultivate my own drive and commitment.

Remember, passion doesn't have to be at a fever pitch from the start. What's important is that you are willing to dig in, learn, and allow your understanding of the industry and your role within it to stoke the flames of passion. This passion can then become the fuel that carries your organization forward, even in the face of challenges.

Passion plays a critical role in startup organizations, particularly when it comes to finance. For startups operating with limited resources and facing significant uncertainty, passion can be a driving force that sustains the team through difficult times.

Internally, it motivates founders and team members to work tirelessly despite financial constraints. This intrinsic motivation can lead to innovative problem-solving and frugality, allowing the startup to stretch its financial resources further. Passionate founders are often willing to take personal financial risks to ensure the startup's survival and growth, fostering a strong company culture driven by a shared vision rather than just financial incentives.

Externally, passion is a key factor in attracting investment. Investors often look for startups led by passionate founders, believing that passion correlates with commitment and the likelihood of success. A passionate pitch can be more persuasive, helping to secure crucial funding, even if the financial projections are not yet solid. Moreover, passion can inspire confidence among customers, partners, and employees, creating a positive feedback loop that enhances the startup's financial stability and growth prospects.

In the high-risk environment of startups, passion is not just a personal trait; it is a vital financial asset. While passion alone is not enough, it can be a powerful catalyst for success when combined with a solid foundation of business acumen, market understanding, and effective execution.

Chapter 4: Fund Raising

"Water shapes its course according to the nature of the ground over which it flows; the soldier works out his victory in relation to the foe whom he is facing."

-Sun Tzu, The Art of War

The landscape of startup funding is a dynamic and critical area for entrepreneurs because securing the necessary capital to launch and grow a business is a significant challenge that can determine the success or failure of a venture. I explore the various funding options available to startups, including traditional routes such as venture capital and angel investment, as well as alternative methods like crowdfunding and bootstrapping.

This is not meant to be a conclusive list or a final determination. You should review and do your own research. There are often opportunities for funding in a specific industry that are unknown to the rest of the world, such as grants, partnerships, and commission structure. At the end of the day, it will be about the relationships you build and cultivate.

When you are in the process of funding research and investor development, remember that all investors have a risk profile. Ask them what this is and adhere to the information they tell you as it relates to the industry interest and the risk profiles. This will allow you to target the right investment at the right time. Also, if this is conducted professionally, even if they have no interest, it will build relationships for the future and for your future partners that may need assistance as well, building the network.

Here are some I will break down in more detail later in the chapter.

Venture Capital: Venture capital (VC) remains a popular option for startups with high growth potential.

Angel Investors: Angel investors are individuals with available capital who invest in early-stage startups.

Bank Loans: Startups with established cash flow and strong financial history may qualify for bank loans.

Initial Public Offering (IPO): An IPO involves selling shares of the company to the public through an investment bank.

Private Placement: Startups can raise equity capital from private investors without going public through a private placement.

Crowdfunding: Crowdfunding platforms enable startups to raise small amounts of money from a large number of individual investors.

Revenue-Based Financing: This model provides funding based on a percentage of the startup's revenue.

Grant Funding: Government agencies, non-profit organizations, and universities often provide grants to startups engaged in innovation, research, or social impact.

Strategic Partnerships: Partnerships with larger companies can provide startups with funding, resources, and market access.

Additional considerations when doing research and selecting a path for funding. Many of these have risks attached as well as benefits; only you and your team will have the ability to create the balance necessary to make the jump forward. Remember that if and when any personal guarantees are requested or required, no matter your corporate structure, you put your personal assets at risk. Be cautious in all finance transactions.

Interest Rate Fluctuations: Rising interest rates can increase the cost of borrowing for startups.

Inflation: Inflation can erode the value of returns on investments.

Capital Availability: Access to capital may fluctuate depending on economic conditions.

Innovation in Financial Technology (FinTech): FinTech is revolutionizing the financial industry.

Navigating the complex fiscal environment requires startups to adopt a comprehensive and flexible approach to finance. By understanding the various debt, equity, and alternative financing options available, startups can tailor their strategies to their specific needs and market conditions. Moreover, embracing innovation in FinTech and staying abreast of economic trends will empower startups to secure sustainable financing and fuel their growth trajectory.

Venture Capital

Venture capital (VC) is one of the most sought-after forms of funding for startups with high growth potential, but it also has its fair share of issues and failures in the overall landscape of capital raising. VC firms are professional investment groups that manage funds and invest in companies with the potential for a significant return on investment (ROI). Often, they seek a rapid ROI, typically within 18 to 24 months, with the goal of multiplying their initial investment significantly.

These VC firms not only provide capital but also offer strategic guidance, networking opportunities, and other valuable resources to the companies in which they invest. However, in exchange for their investment, they usually require a portion of equity in the company. The investment process often involves multiple stages, from seed funding to Series A, B, and beyond.

Through personal experience, the author has observed that VCs tend to invest in opportunities that are recommended by their friends and fellow VCs. They are often unwilling to invest solely in a venture, preferring to "partner" with other investors and spread the risk across multiple investments. This approach is reminiscent of the casino model, where the house (the VCs) aims to bet on winning ventures and ensure that they always come out on top.

Overall, the passage highlights the complexities and dynamics involved in the VC funding landscape, where startups with high growth potential navigate the challenges of securing investments while VC firms carefully manage their portfolios to maximize returns.

Stages of Venture Capital Funding:

Seed Funding: Initial capital to develop a prototype or conduct market research. It is a rare opportunity for a VC to do a seed round. So, do not expect to have a lot of traction with this type of investor as a seed investment partner; it does happen, but rarely.

Series A: Funding to scale the business and develop a customer base. When a VC enters this type of round, they expect that you are cash flowing, and if so, when will it be a positive cash flow, and that you have significant customer acquisition and foundational growth.

Series B and Beyond: Additional rounds to expand operations, enter new markets, and achieve profitability. Many times, if you look at this stage, you would be cash flow positive, and the additional investment would be an exit strategy, such as an IPO, or accelerated growth needs, such as a new distribution center or factory.

Pros:

- Large amounts of capital
- Strategic guidance and resources
- Credibility and validation

Cons:

- Significant equity dilution
- High expectations for growth and returns
- Potential loss of control

Angel Investors

Angel investors are affluent individuals who provide capital for startups, often in exchange for convertible debt or ownership equity. Unlike VCs, angel investors use their personal funds and may take a less active role in the company. They are often driven by their interest in the business or the entrepreneur themselves and can be a valuable source of funding during the early stages of a company's growth. In this category, a question that you should ask is how the last investment they made was, the results, the expectations, the time duration, involvement, and any expected exit strategies that they need to see.

I have found that many Angelers invest less frequently and in fewer amounts per year, so understanding the last investment may be critical to when and if they will invest in your opportunity.

Who Are Angel Investors? Angel investors are wealthy individuals who provide capital to startups in exchange for equity. They often have experience in the industry and can offer valuable mentorship and networking opportunities. They, in most cases, look at specific industries and sectors; they are more focused on the team and the personal benefits to their portfolio, bragging rights.

How to Find Them: Angel investors can be found through networking events, online platforms like AngelList, and industry connections. They will need face-to-face meetings; they are all about the relationship and the "breaking of bread" type of relationship.

Pros of Angel Investment:

- Significant capital infusion, but on a less frequent basis and maybe in a step approach rather than a large amount. So, you may see a term sheet for an amount, but it will be regulated by performance rather than time.
- Mentorship and industry expertise
- Networking opportunities

Cons of Angel Investment:

- Equity dilution
- High return expectations
- Potential loss of control
- May require more personal involvement and a hands-on approach, which may create tension within your team. Know who the person(s) is and any history, and do your research because they will be involved in your business.
- May require a personal guarantee that puts your personal assets at risk

Crowdfunding

Crowdfunding is a way of raising capital through the collective effort of friends, family, customers, and individual investors. This approach taps into the collective efforts of a large pool of individuals—primarily online via social media and crowdfunding platforms—and leverages their networks for greater reach and exposure. Crowdfunding can be a useful tool for startups not only to raise funds but also to validate the product and build a community of supporters.

With current regulations and opportunities, you can investigate the SEC, Securities and Exchange Commission, crowdfunding options such as Reg D, and others as a way to build smaller investment pools and leverage marketing reach. All crowdfunding is like any other option; it will take marketing and work to get the job done. It will not happen on its own.

For example, some Reg D offerings may require as many as several hundred thousand dollars in order to raise several million. It might be a great investment, but be aware of all of the costs and processes related to this type of fundraising; it can be costly as an upfront investment.

Types of Crowdfunding:

Donation-Based: Supporters donate money without expecting anything in return.

Reward-Based: Backers receive a product or service in return for their contribution.

Equity-Based: Investors receive equity in the company in exchange for their investment.

Popular Platforms: Kickstarter, Indiegogo, GoFundMe, and Crowdcube are some of the well-known crowdfunding platforms.

Pros of Crowdfunding:

- Access to a large pool of potential backers
- Market validation and customer engagement
- No need to repay funds (in reward-based crowdfunding)

Cons of Crowdfunding:

- Requires significant marketing effort
- Platform fees and costs
- Potential for public failure
- A larger investor pool to manage, you might need a person in charge of investor relations at this point.
- The cost to market, structure, and offer, such as PPM and Offering documents, could be costly for a startup. Be aware that all the costs are known prior to being a campaign; it is all about marketing when you start a crowdfunding campaign.

Bootstrapping

Bootstrapping is when an entrepreneur starts a company with little capital, relying on personal savings and revenue from the business to support its growth. This method forces the entrepreneur to be resourceful and frugal, which can be a strong foundation for building a disciplined company culture. While this approach can limit the speed of growth, it allows founders to maintain full control over their business.

This involves using personal savings, reinvesting profits, and minimizing expenses to grow the business. While it fosters financial discipline and independence, it can limit the speed and scale of growth due to limited resources.

Pros **of Bootstrapping**:

- Full control over the business
- No debt or equity dilution
- Encourages financial discipline

Cons of Bootstrapping:

- Limited capital
- High personal financial risk
- Slower growth potential

Friends and Family/ Informal Loans:

Borrowing money from friends and family can be a quick and flexible way to raise funds. These loans often come with lower interest rates and more lenient repayment terms. In the process of getting investments and loans from this type of investor, you should treat them just like any other investor. Perform due diligence, have firm contracts, be aware of risk profiles, and never take money that may impact a member of this group negatively.

Ask questions like, can they still pay the bills if the investment does not work out, can they afford the investment with risk to their own portfolio, can they have the patience to wait for a return, and will it affect your relationship with the person or persons?

Friends and family may also invest in exchange for equity in the company. This can provide significant capital without the need for immediate repayment. This can be done on a Promissory Note style contract, a promise to pay with a potential for conversion to stock or equity in the firm.

Pros of Informal Loans:

- Flexible terms
- Lower interest rates
- Quick access to funds

Cons of Informal Loans:

- Potential for strained relationships
- Lack of formal agreements
- Limited funding amounts

Small Business Loans

Traditional Bank Loans: Banks offer various loan products, including term loans, lines of credit, and equipment financing. These loans typically require good credit and collateral. In my experience, they will lend you money as long as the risk is very little, almost none. They like to lend when you really don't need the cash, and as a startup, they, in most cases, will require a personal guarantee that will encumber all of your assets. Additionally, they will look at cash flow, company assets, time in business, and purchase orders to lessen their risk in the loan process.

- **SBA Loans**: The Small Business Administration (SBA) offers loan programs that provide guarantees to lenders, making it easier for small businesses to obtain financing. This is a great opportunity, but it has issues. They will require time in business and cash on hand, usually 15% of the requested amount. The SBA is a guarantor of loans, and your actual loan will come from an authorized lender in the standard backing industry, so the requirements will be the same as those of a standard loan.

- **Online Lenders**: Online platforms like Kabbage and OnDeck offer quick and flexible loan options, often with less stringent requirements than traditional banks. These can be an option; be aware of fees, broker fees, application fees, and all details of this option. Some online organizations make their money on application fees and never really do many loans if any at all. Again, do your research, ask questions, and look at references.

Pros of Small Business Loans:

- Access to substantial capital
- Fixed repayment terms
- Retain full ownership

Cons of Small Business Loans:

- Requires good credit and collateral
- Interest and fees
- Lengthy application process

Grants

Government Grants: Various government agencies offer grants to support small businesses, particularly those in specific industries or with innovative products. In many regions, governments offer grants and loans to support startups, particularly in sectors that are strategically important or innovative.

These funding sources can be highly beneficial as they often come with lower interest rates and favorable terms. However, they can also be competitive and require strict adherence to guidelines and reporting. Grants, in some cases, are just that: grants with no repayment necessary, but they always have strings attached.

In most grants, the money is allocated according to the grant designs, with no variation. So, if it says you can only do research, then that is all you can do. If you do anything other than that, they have the potential to recall all of the funds, so be aware.

Additionally, most grants require time in business, some as much as three years. Why? They want to understand your track record and the service impacts of what you do and how you do it.

There are hundreds, maybe thousands, of people who can get grants written for you and help in the application process. These people utilize not only the application process and writing skills but also relationships.

They will typically write a grant to and for an industry that they have had success in the past, so look for specific grant writers with targeted experiences.

These skilled professionals will need to get paid upfront for the work they will do. There is no guarantee of success, so they want cash, and there may be a success fee due upon the award of a grant. Read all the documents fully before going down this path. Foundations and corporations also provide grants to support entrepreneurship and innovation.

Pros of Grants:

- No need to repay funds
- Can provide significant capital
- Recognition and credibility

Cons of Grants:

- Highly competitive
- Strict eligibility criteria
- Lengthy application process
- No guarantee of award and funding

Business Incubators and Accelerators

What They Offer: Incubators and accelerators provide funding, mentorship, office space, and resources to help startups grow. Incubators typically focus on early-stage companies, while accelerators help more developed startups scale quickly. This is a great way to break into business ownership. In many cases, there will be shared resources, a group setting, and shared knowledge from the group. So, this shared knowledge, relationships, contacts, networks, and resources lessen the stress of the unknown.

How to Apply: Applications usually involve submitting a business plan and pitch deck and participating in interviews or pitch events. Some incubators can and will help in the application process, such as the pitch deck and business foundational work.

In some cases, the application requires an investment and a commitment to the organization. So, again, be aware of all of the contracts and obligations that are required before you get involved. They can be great, but also they can take away much-needed cash flow.

I support and encourage these organizations all the time. I was on the advisory board of a few where over 1500 new businesses were taking part; that is a great wealth of knowledge and excitement that can be tapped into for your organization.

Pros of Business Incubators and Accelerators:

- Access to funding and resources
- Mentorship and networking
- Accelerated growth

Cons of Business Incubators and Accelerators:

- Equity dilution
- Intensive programs
- Potential relocation

Alternative Financing Options

Don't let the name alternative set you back. This opportunity is where you can get creative with your funding request, design, and outcomes. I like partnerships in this type of funding process, as well as synergistic and strategic partnerships. If an organization that is aligned with you can help raise the level of your business through supply chain, inventory, lower costs, or access, then it may be a great partnership.

Let me give you an example: Let's say you are going to manufacture a steel product, and your supplier will sell you all you need at retail, and that is fine. But, if you find a partner with another firm that utilizes the same supplier, you might be able to use their credit line and have access to purchase the items at a much lower cost and with greater ease of delivery. It is all about leveraging your network and contacts to lower cast, leverage investments, and build long-term relationships.

- **Peer-to-Peer Lending**: Platforms like LendingClub and Prosper connect borrowers with individual lenders, offering flexible loan terms and competitive rates.
- **Revenue-Based Financing**: Companies like Lighter Capital provide funding in exchange for a percentage of future revenue rather than equity or fixed repayments.
- **Asset-Based Financing**: Loans secured by company assets, such as inventory or accounts receivable, can provide quick access to capital.

Pros:

- Flexible terms
- Quick access to funds
- No equity dilution

Cons:

- Higher interest rates and fees
- Risk of losing assets
- Limited funding amounts

Future Outlook for Startup Financing

As we look ahead, the global startup financing landscape is set to undergo a remarkable transformation, brimming with exciting new trends and innovative financing models. While the past has shown us the challenges and complexities inherent in securing funding, the future promises a world of opportunities for aspiring entrepreneurs.

One of the key drivers of this evolution will be the rapid advancements in technology, which are set to redefine the way startups access and manage their finances. Cutting-edge fintech solutions, blockchain-based platforms, and data-driven analytics are poised to revolutionize the traditional funding paradigm, making it more accessible, transparent, and efficient.

Moreover, the emergence of new financing models, such as crowdfunding platforms, revenue-based financing, and crypto-based instruments, will continue to democratize the startup funding ecosystem. These alternative avenues will empower entrepreneurs to explore a diverse range of options tailored to their unique needs and growth trajectories.

Alongside these technological and financial innovations, we can also expect to see a greater emphasis on sustainability, social impact, and ethical investment practices. Investors and funders alike will increasingly prioritize startups that align with these values, creating a more holistic and purpose-driven startup ecosystem.

As we navigate this exciting future, one thing is certain: the key to success will lie in embracing the spirit of innovation, adaptability, and a deep understanding of the ever-evolving funding landscape. By staying informed, building strategic partnerships, and leveraging the power of emerging technologies, startups can position themselves for long-term success and unlock the boundless potential that lies ahead.

The global and domestic economic environment has significantly changed in recent years, deeply affecting the startup ecosystem. Pandemics, for instance, can cause massive disruptions across industries, leading to a reevaluation of business models and investment strategies. Although the initial impact was severe, the pandemic also catalyzed innovation, with many startups pivoting to meet new market demands.

Geopolitical tensions, such as those between the United States and China, have also impacted global trade and investment flows. These tensions have created uncertainty, particularly for startups operating in or relying on global supply chains. Additionally, trade policies and tariffs have increased operational costs, making it harder for startups to compete on an international scale.

Inflation and rising interest rates have further complicated the financial landscape. Central banks around the world have raised interest rates to combat inflation, increasing the cost of borrowing. This environment has made traditional bank loans less accessible and more expensive for startups, pushing them to seek alternative financing methods.

Regional economic disparities have also influenced startup financing. While regions like North America and Western Europe continue to attract substantial investment, emerging markets face significant challenges in securing capital. Factors such as political instability, weak financial infrastructure, and limited access to international markets have constrained the growth of startups in these regions.

Technology Startups

Technology startups continue to dominate the global startup landscape, attracting significant investment due to their potential for rapid growth and scalability. AI and blockchain are two of the most prominent areas within tech, with substantial funding flowing into startups developing AI-driven solutions and blockchain-based platforms.

The growing importance of data and cybersecurity has also led to increased investments in these areas.

Investors are keenly aware of the rising demand for secure and efficient data management solutions, especially in an era of increasing cyber threats.

Biotech and Healthcare Startups

Biotech and healthcare startups have seen a surge in investment, particularly in the wake of the COVID-19 pandemic. The urgent need for medical innovation, coupled with advancements in genomics, personalized medicine, and telehealth, has attracted significant capital. However, the sector also faces unique challenges, including lengthy regulatory approval processes and high R&D costs.

Green and Sustainable Startups

The global push toward sustainability has led to a boom in green startups, particularly those focused on renewable energy, waste reduction, and sustainable agriculture. ESG considerations are playing an increasingly important role in investment decisions, with investors seeking to support companies that contribute positively to environmental and social outcomes.

Startups in the circular economy and those developing sustainable products and services are receiving growing attention. However, these companies often face challenges related to scaling and the need for significant upfront capital.

Fintech Startups

Fintech startups have been at the forefront of innovation, disrupting traditional financial services with digital solutions. The sector has attracted substantial investment, driven by the increasing adoption of digital payments, blockchain, and financial inclusion initiatives. However, regulatory challenges and the need to comply with varying legal frameworks across different regions pose significant hurdles.

The rise of embedded finance, where financial services are integrated into non-financial platforms, represents a key trend within fintech. Startups in this space are increasingly securing funding as they offer innovative solutions that meet the needs of modern consumers.

Market Volatility and Its Impact

One of the main challenges facing startups is market volatility, which can significantly impact investor confidence. Economic downturns, geopolitical instability, and global health crises can lead to a tightening of available capital, making it difficult for startups to secure the necessary funding to grow.

Valuation Concerns and the Search for Sustainable Growth

Valuation concerns have also become more prominent, particularly in tech sectors where startups may be overvalued based on speculative future growth. This can lead to difficulties in securing later-stage funding or achieving successful exits.

Access to Capital in Emerging Markets

Access to capital remains a significant barrier for startups in emerging markets. Despite the growing interest in these regions, challenges such as political instability, underdeveloped financial infrastructure, and limited access to global markets continue to hinder the flow of investment.

Opportunities in the Evolving Financing Landscape

Despite these challenges, there are several opportunities for startups in the current financing landscape. The ongoing digital transformation across industries has created new business models and markets, offering startups the chance to capitalize on emerging trends.

Globalization of Startup Finance

The globalization of startup finance has also opened up new avenues for cross-border investments. Startups in emerging markets, for example, are increasingly attracting international investors looking for high-growth opportunities.

Innovative Financing Instruments and Technologies

New financial instruments and technologies are also creating opportunities for startups. The rise of DeFi, for example, is providing startups with alternative ways to raise capital without relying on traditional financial institutions.

The Role of Startup Support Ecosystems

Incubators, accelerators, and startup hubs play a crucial role in supporting the growth and development of startups. These organizations provide startups with essential resources, including mentorship, networking opportunities, and access to capital.

Global Startup Hubs and Successful Ecosystems

Global startup hubs such as Silicon Valley, London, and Beijing continue to be magnets for startups and investors alike. These hubs offer a unique ecosystem that fosters innovation and provides startups with the support they need to succeed. Case studies of successful startup ecosystems, such as Israel's "Startup Nation" and India's burgeoning tech scene, demonstrate the importance of a supportive environment in nurturing startups.

The Influence of Government Policies and Regulations

Government policies and regulations play a significant role in shaping the startup financing landscape. In many countries, governments have introduced measures to support startups, including tax incentives, grants, and favorable regulatory frameworks. However, regulatory challenges remain, particularly for startups operating in highly regulated industries such as fintech and healthcare.

The Role of International Organizations

International organizations, such as the World Bank and the International Monetary Fund (IMF), also play a role in shaping the global startup financing landscape. These organizations provide funding and support to startups in developing countries, helping to bridge the gap between local startups and global investors.

The Future of Startup Financing

The future of startup financing is likely to be shaped by several key trends. The continued growth of digital technologies and the increasing importance of sustainability are expected to drive investment in these areas. Startups that can capitalize on these trends are likely to attract significant funding. Emerging markets are also expected to play a more prominent role in the global startup ecosystem, offering significant growth opportunities for both startups and investors. The rise of new financial instruments and technologies, such as DeFi and blockchain-based financing, is likely to continue, providing startups with alternative ways to raise capital.

Embracing the Evolving Landscape

The current status of finance for startups in the global economy is characterized by a complex and dynamic landscape. While challenges such as market volatility, valuation concerns, and access to capital in emerging markets persist, there are also significant opportunities for startups. By staying informed of the latest trends and developments in startup financing, entrepreneurs, investors, and policymakers can better navigate the challenges and capitalize on the opportunities in this exciting and rapidly evolving sector.

Chapter 5: Jumping off the Ledge and Getting Started

If you know yourself but not the enemy, for every victory gained, you will also suffer a defeat.

If you know neither the enemy nor yourself, you will succumb in every battle.

-Sun Tzu, The Art of War

Entrepreneurs today are operating in a vastly different environment compared to just a few decades ago, primarily due to the surge of technological tools, resources, and networks that have become available. When I started my first business in the late 70s, we had limited resources – some basic tools and the drive to make money. As my entrepreneurial journey progressed, I was able to leverage emerging technologies and business development opportunities, unlocking a new landscape of possibilities.

The rise of the internet and the expansion of digital platforms have made access to information and resources more democratic, which was once the exclusive domain of large corporations. For example, cloud computing services such as Amazon Web Services (AWS) and Google Cloud offer startups scalable infrastructure at a fraction of the cost of traditional IT setups. This allows even the smallest companies to start and manage operations without needing significant upfront capital. Additionally, the availability of advanced software tools for tasks like project management (such as Asana or Trello) and customer relationship management (like Salesforce) has streamlined business processes, enabling startups to operate more efficiently and focus on innovation.

However, it's important to understand the short-term and long-term implications of technological decisions. Factors like licensing issues, copyrights, use permits, and other legal considerations need to be carefully evaluated. These aspects can significantly contribute to a startup's overall operational budget and have far-reaching consequences. Technology can be a valuable tool, but it can also become a burden if not managed wisely.

The rise of social media and digital marketing has also transformed how startups connect with customers and build brands. Platforms like Instagram, Facebook, LinkedIn, and TikTok allow companies to reach global audiences with minimal marketing budgets, a stark contrast to the costly advertising campaigns required in the past. While the use of social media has become ubiquitous in business today, it's crucial to ensure that you are not only leveraging technological intelligence but also emotional intelligence across your digital platforms. A lack of intelligence in the utilization of social media can render an organization incapacitated and unable to recover. This democratization of marketing has leveled the playing field, allowing even small startups to compete with established brands on a global scale. Additionally, online marketplaces such as Amazon, Etsy, and Shopify have provided entrepreneurs with the tools to sell products directly to consumers worldwide, bypassing traditional retail channels.

The availability of educational resources has also improved dramatically, empowering entrepreneurs to access a wealth of knowledge through online courses, webinars, and digital libraries. Platforms like Coursera, Udemy, and Khan Academy offer courses on entrepreneurship, finance, marketing, and technology, providing individuals with the skills they need to start and grow their businesses.

Startup incubators and accelerators, such as Y Combinator, Techstars, and 500 Startups, have also emerged as valuable resources, offering structured support, mentorship, and funding to help startups navigate the challenges of early-stage growth. Initiatives like our own E=MC22 Innovation Centers can provide a great starting point for organizations, connecting them with industry experts who are willing to offer guidance, advice, and potentially even equity investments.

The global network of investors, mentors, and fellow entrepreneurs has expanded significantly, facilitated by the internet and global connectivity. Entrepreneurs can now participate in online communities, attend virtual conferences, and engage with a broader network of professionals who can provide advice, funding, and partnership opportunities. Platforms like LinkedIn have become essential tools for networking, allowing entrepreneurs to connect with potential investors, partners, and customers across the globe. Leveraging this network can be a powerful advantage, though it's important to discern which advice and connections are truly valuable rather than becoming overwhelmed.

The motivation behind starting new companies today is often driven by a desire to innovate and address pressing global challenges. Entrepreneurs are increasingly aware of the impact their businesses can have on society and the environment, leading to a rise in social entrepreneurship and purpose-driven companies. These entrepreneurs are not only focused on profit but also on creating solutions that address issues like climate change, inequality, and public health.

The availability of funding specifically targeted at social impact startups, such as impact investing funds, has further encouraged the growth of businesses that aim to make a positive difference in the world. While this passion for creating positive change is commendable, it's crucial that entrepreneurs maintain a balanced perspective, ensuring they don't become too narrowly focused on their cause at the expense of other critical business aspects. Seeking out diverse perspectives and expert guidance can help entrepreneurs navigate this balance effectively.

The resilience required to succeed in today's dynamic and competitive global market is truly formidable. Entrepreneurs must be adaptable and ready to pivot their business models in response to rapid market changes, economic downturns, or unexpected challenges that can spill over into their marketplace. However, it is this very resilience that lays the foundation for long-term success.

Entrepreneurs who can navigate these challenges are often better positioned to capitalize on new opportunities and sustain their businesses over time. The ability to innovate, adapt, and persevere in the face of adversity not only helps startups survive but also thrive in an ever-evolving global economy. This resilience is a critical differentiator, as it enables entrepreneurs to overcome setbacks and emerge stronger on the other side.

Fortunately, the entrepreneurial ecosystem has evolved to provide greater support to those who possess this resilience. Governments, private organizations, and educational institutions have recognized the vital role that startups play in driving economic growth and innovation. As a result, they have developed policies, programs, and initiatives to support entrepreneurs, providing them with access to capital, mentorship, and a wealth of resources.

This supportive environment, combined with the ever-expanding tools and networks now available, has empowered more individuals than ever to take the leap into entrepreneurship. They can do so with greater confidence, knowing that they have the resources and resilience to succeed. In this way, today's entrepreneurs are not just building businesses; they are shaping the future of the global economy, leveraging their adaptability and tenacity to bring innovative solutions to the market.

The resilience required to navigate the modern entrepreneurial landscape is a true testament to the determination and vision of today's startup founders. By embracing this resilience and capitalizing on the supportive ecosystem, entrepreneurs are poised to drive transformative change, weather any storm, and ultimately leave an indelible mark on the global economic landscape.

Why Start a New Company in Today's Finance Market?

Starting a new company in today's financial market might seem daunting given the economic uncertainties, fluctuating interest rates, and the volatile global landscape. However, the current market also presents unique opportunities for entrepreneurs who are ready to navigate these complexities.

The allure of entrepreneurship has not waned; if anything, it has been fueled by the digital revolution, the rise of new financial instruments, and the evolving needs of consumers. The key reasons individuals might start a new company in today's financial market are the opportunities presented by technological advancements, access to diverse financing options, the demand for innovative solutions, and the broader socio-economic shifts driving entrepreneurial activity.

1. Technological Advancements

One of the most compelling reasons to start a new company today is the unprecedented access to cutting-edge technology. The rapid development of digital tools, platforms, and infrastructure has lowered the barriers to entry for aspiring entrepreneurs.

Technologies like artificial intelligence (AI), blockchain, and cloud computing have democratized innovation, enabling even small startups to develop products and services that were once the domain of large corporations.

For example, the proliferation of cloud computing allows startups to scale their operations quickly without the need for significant upfront investment in physical infrastructure. This means that a tech startup can develop a global presence from day one, leveraging cloud services to deliver their product or service to a worldwide audience.

Artificial intelligence and machine learning are also transforming industries, providing startups with the ability to create smarter, more personalized products. Whether it's through AI-driven customer service, predictive analytics, or automated processes, new companies can harness these technologies to gain a competitive edge.

Moreover, the rise of low-code and no-code platforms has enabled entrepreneurs without extensive technical backgrounds to create sophisticated software applications. This democratization of technology means that more people than ever before have the tools to bring their ideas to life, leading to a surge in startup activity across various sectors.

2. Diverse Financing Options

The wide array of financing options available to entrepreneurs today is a key reason for starting a new company. The traditional venture capital (VC) model is still very much in play, but it is now complemented by a diverse range of alternative funding sources that cater to different needs and stages of business development.

While the VC market does hold a wealth of wisdom, it's important to recognize that it may not always be the best or most accessible starting point, especially for new startups without a proven track record of disruptive innovation. There are many other avenues worth exploring, and I'm glad you plan to delve into these in more detail in the following chapters.

I will discuss these more in the following chapters. The list is not complete nor exclusive. Use your imagination and network to find all the options available to you and your organization. Finance is the main reason I began the adventure of writing this book, and we are frustrated with the current models.

In my several decades of hunting for money for our organizations and many others, from cold fusion to golf club companies, I have learned a lot, and I want to share that education with you and your organization.

Venture Capital and Angel Investing:

Venture capital continues to be a crucial source of funding, particularly for startups operating in high-growth sectors such as technology, biotech, and fintech. Despite the inherent risks, VCs remain committed to investing in innovative startups with the potential to disrupt industries and deliver substantial returns. These deep-pocketed investors bring not only capital but also invaluable industry expertise and mentorship to the table.

Complementing the VC model, angel investors play a critical role in providing early-stage funding to startups. These individual investors often possess significant experience and connections within their respective fields, and they leverage this knowledge to identify promising opportunities and nurture fledgling businesses. The guidance and backing of angel investors can be instrumental in helping startups navigate the challenges of the early stages of growth.

While the venture capital and angel investor landscapes carry an element of risk, the potential rewards make them appealing avenues for entrepreneurs seeking to scale their businesses and capitalize on emerging market trends. Startups that are able to capture the attention of these influential financiers can gain access to the resources, networks, and strategic insights needed to accelerate their growth and disrupt established industries.

It’s worth noting, however, that these traditional funding sources may not be the best fit for every entrepreneur or every stage of a company’s development. The startup financing landscape has evolved to include a diverse array of alternative options, each with its own unique characteristics and suitability for different business models and growth stages.

Savvy entrepreneurs should carefully evaluate the various financing alternatives available to them and select the approach that aligns most closely with their goals, risk tolerance, and long-term vision.

By understanding the nuances of the venture capital and angel investor ecosystems, as well as the emergence of alternative financing solutions, entrepreneurs can maximize their chances of securing the capital and support needed to transform their bold ideas into thriving, industry-disrupting enterprises.

Crowdfunding:

Crowdfunding platforms like Kickstarter and Indiegogo have democratized access to capital, empowering entrepreneurs to raise funds directly from the public. This innovative model not only provides the necessary financial backing but also serves as a valuable market validation tool. By engaging with potential customers and gauging their interest and demand for a product or service before it is fully developed, entrepreneurs can better assess the viability of their business idea and make more informed decisions.

The crowdfunding approach offers several advantages over traditional funding sources. It allows entrepreneurs to bypass the gatekeepers of venture capital and angel investing, giving them the opportunity to connect directly with a broader pool of supporters. Additionally, a successful crowdfunding campaign can generate valuable buzz and visibility for the startup, helping to build a loyal customer base even before the product or service is launched.

Perhaps most importantly, crowdfunding platforms enable entrepreneurs to test the market and validate their assumptions in real-time. The feedback and financial commitments received during the crowdfunding process can provide invaluable insights, allowing founders to refine their offerings, identify pain points, and better align their products or services with the needs of their target audience.

Over the years, development has led the crowdfunding process to a very professional level. The utilization of SEC compliance and other laws that have been formed around this type of funding has allowed the new organization to be in the position to raise as much as 75 million, under the correct formats, in initial funding, such as Regulation D 506a and other methods.

By embracing the democratized nature of crowdfunding, entrepreneurs can gain access to capital, gauge market interest, and strengthen their connection with potential customers – all while maintaining greater control over their business's development and direction. This powerful combination of funding and market validation can be a critical factor in the long-term success of startups operating in today's dynamic and highly competitive business landscape.

Revenue-Based Financing and Alternative Lending:

Revenue-based financing has emerged as a flexible alternative to traditional equity financing. In this model, startups receive capital in exchange for a percentage of their future revenue, enabling them to secure the necessary funds for growth while retaining ownership of their business. This approach can be particularly appealing to entrepreneurs who are reluctant to dilute their equity or who may not meet the stringent requirements of traditional venture capital or angel investors.

Complementing the rise of revenue-based financing, alternative lending platforms have also gained traction in the startup financing landscape. These platforms often offer more accessible loan options with less stringent requirements compared to traditional banking institutions. By leveraging data-driven underwriting models and innovative lending strategies, these alternative lenders are able to cater to the unique needs and challenges of early-stage startups, providing them with the capital and financial support necessary to scale their operations.

By diversifying the funding landscape, these innovative financing solutions empower entrepreneurs to navigate the startup journey with greater flexibility and control. This, in turn, can foster an environment of increased innovation, as founders are empowered to pursue their visions without being overly constrained by the limitations of traditional financing structures.

Cryptocurrency and Blockchain-Based Financing:

The rise of cryptocurrencies and blockchain technology has opened up new avenues for startup financing. Initial Coin Offerings (ICOs), Security Token Offerings (STOs), and Decentralized Finance (DeFi) platforms offer innovative ways to raise capital without relying on traditional financial institutions. These methods are particularly attractive to tech-savvy entrepreneurs and those developing blockchain-based solutions.

This diverse range of financing options means that entrepreneurs can tailor their funding strategy to their specific needs, whether they require seed capital to get started or growth capital to scale their operations.

3. Demand for Innovative Solutions

The ever-changing global landscape, shaped by technological advancements, shifting consumer preferences, and socio-economic changes, has created a strong demand for innovative solutions. Entrepreneurs who can identify and address emerging needs have a significant opportunity to build successful companies.

Health and Wellness: The COVID-19 pandemic has heightened awareness of health and wellness, leading to increased demand for products and services that promote physical and mental well-being. Startups in telehealth, fitness tech, and mental health apps are thriving as consumers prioritize their health in new ways.

Sustainability and Green Technology: Climate change and environmental concerns are driving demand for sustainable products and services. Green startups focused on renewable energy, sustainable agriculture, and eco-friendly consumer goods are well-positioned to capitalize on this trend. Investors are also increasingly prioritizing Environmental, Social, and Governance (ESG) factors, providing additional incentives for startups in this space.

Digital Transformation: Businesses across industries are undergoing digital transformation to stay competitive. This shift creates opportunities for startups that offer digital solutions, whether it's through software as a service (SaaS), e-commerce platforms, or digital marketing tools. The need for remote work solutions, cybersecurity, and data analytics has also surged, providing fertile ground for new companies.

Consumer Personalization: Today's consumers expect personalized experiences tailored to their individual needs and preferences. Startups that leverage data and AI to create customized products and services are in high demand. This trend is evident in industries such as retail, entertainment, and financial services, where companies are increasingly using technology to deliver unique experiences.

The ability to innovate and adapt to these evolving demands is a powerful motivator for entrepreneurs. By staying attuned to market trends and consumer needs, startups can carve out niches and build strong brands that resonate with their target audiences. In my consulting, I look for opportunities, and they are everywhere you look. It is about situational awareness and acting, jumping, and taking advantage of an opportunity when you can. The ability to adapt to what you are doing with new visions and offerings makes you stand out from the one-trick-pony syndrome that is the bane of many startups.

4. Socio-Economic Shifts Driving Entrepreneurship

Beyond technology and market demand, broader socio-economic shifts are also contributing to the rise of new companies. These shifts are changing how people think about work, business, and the economy, creating a fertile environment for entrepreneurship. We talk about this part of business with a lot of buzzwords and analogies. The point is always to be aware and look; the global community is available for your offerings, so reach out and discover.

The Gig Economy and Freelancing:

The gig economy has reshaped the traditional employment landscape, with more people opting for freelance work and independent contracting. This shift has lowered the barriers to starting a business as individuals increasingly seek to leverage their skills and expertise through entrepreneurial ventures. The flexibility of the gig economy also encourages the development of side businesses, which can eventually grow into full-fledged companies.

Globalization and Remote Work:

Globalization has made it easier for startups to access international markets, suppliers, and talent. The rise of remote work, accelerated by the pandemics, world economies, shifting governmental attitudes, and political aspirations, has further enabled startups to build distributed teams and operate across borders. This global connectivity means that entrepreneurs are no longer constrained by their geographic location, allowing them to tap into global opportunities and markets.

The Rise of Social Entrepreneurship:

There is a growing interest in businesses that address social, environmental, and economic challenges. Social entrepreneurs are driven by the desire to make a positive impact, and they often attract like-minded investors and customers who prioritize purpose-driven business. The rise of social entrepreneurship is supported by the increasing availability of impact investment funds, which seek to generate both financial returns and positive societal outcomes.

Changing Attitudes Toward Risk:

The perception of risk has evolved, with many people now viewing entrepreneurship as a viable and attractive career path. This shift is partly due to the success stories of high-profile entrepreneurs who have built multi-billion-dollar companies from scratch. The glamorization of startup culture, coupled with the availability of resources and support networks, has made entrepreneurship more accessible and appealing.

These socio-economic trends are reshaping the entrepreneurial landscape, making it more inclusive and diverse. As a result, a wider range of individuals are starting new companies, driven by a combination of personal motivations and the desire to create meaningful change.

5. Resilience in the Face of Uncertainty

While starting a new company in today's financial market comes with its challenges, it also offers the opportunity to build resilience in the face of uncertainty. The ability to adapt and innovate during turbulent times can lead to long-term success and growth.

Economic Downturns as Opportunities:

Economic downturns often lead to the emergence of new businesses as entrepreneurs identify gaps in the market and respond to changing consumer needs. Recessions can also lead to a more favorable environment for startups, as larger companies may scale back operations, leaving room for new entrants.

The Importance of Agility:

Startups are inherently agile and can pivot more quickly than established companies. This agility is crucial in today's fast-paced market, where conditions can change rapidly. Entrepreneurs who can adapt to new challenges and seize opportunities are more likely to succeed in the long term.

Building Resilient Business Models:

Entrepreneurs today are increasingly focused on building resilient business models that can withstand economic shocks. This includes diversifying revenue streams, leveraging technology to reduce costs, and creating flexible business structures that can adapt to changing conditions.

The resilience that comes from navigating a challenging financial environment can ultimately strengthen a startup, positioning it for future success. Entrepreneurs who can weather the storms of uncertainty are often better equipped to capitalize on opportunities as they arise.

Be aware of the conversations and meetings that you participate in. There will always be those who turn a blind eye to your innovations, but there will also be those who are hungry to support your efforts. Learn from the naysayers and team up with the supporters.

Starting a new company in today's financial market offers a unique blend of challenges and opportunities. Technological advancements, diverse financing options, the demand for innovative solutions, and broader socio-economic shifts all create a favorable environment for entrepreneurship. While the financial market may be unpredictable, the potential rewards for those who can navigate its complexities are significant.

Whether motivated by the desire to innovate, solve pressing global challenges, or create a business that reflects their personal values, individuals are increasingly choosing to start new companies. The resilience required to succeed in today's market may be formidable, but it also lays the foundation for long-term success in an ever-evolving global economy.

In the heat of an idea, when we spot an opportunity driven by a particular situation or thought, the temptation to create a new organization can be strong. We may believe that we can do better than those who have come before us, but that is not always the case. In my experience, new ideas can arise quite frequently, sometimes as often as every 45 minutes or less. However, it is not just the idea itself that matters, but rather the projected outcome and the myriad of factors that will ultimately determine its success – factors that may not be immediately apparent.

Factors such as the strength of the team, access to funding, market conditions, and countless other considerations will all play a crucial role in determining whether an idea can be successfully translated into a thriving business. The pursuit of financial independence and the aspiration to create impactful change within an industry can certainly be motivating factors, but they alone do not guarantee success.

That said, the current market conditions do present opportunities for disruption. Entrepreneurs who are willing to stir the pot and take calculated risks can capture the attention of both consumers and potential investors. With consumers increasingly seeking personalized experiences, new companies can capitalize on this trend by offering tailored financial products that cater to specific needs. This level of customization is often beyond the scope of larger, more established firms, giving startups a competitive edge.

Furthermore, the regulatory environment has become more favorable for new entrants in the finance market. Governments and regulatory bodies are recognizing the importance of innovation in finance and are creating frameworks that encourage the growth of startups. This supportive regulatory landscape can significantly reduce barriers to entry and operational risks for new companies, making it a more inviting environment for entrepreneurs to thrive.

While the temptation to act on a new idea can be strong, it is essential to carefully consider the broader context and the myriad of factors that will ultimately determine the success or failure of a new venture. By approaching the pursuit of a new organization with a clear-eyed understanding of the challenges and opportunities, entrepreneurs can increase their chances of creating a truly impactful and sustainable enterprise.

Starting a new company in the finance sector also allows for greater agility and adaptability. Unlike larger, more established corporations, startups possess the flexibility to pivot and iterate their business models rapidly in response to market feedback. This nimbleness is crucial in the finance market, where consumer preferences and regulatory landscapes can shift swiftly, creating both challenges and opportunities.

In addition to these market-driven factors, personal motivations play a significant role in the decision to start an entrepreneurial journey. Entrepreneurship offers a sense of autonomy and the ability to directly impact the success of the business. For many aspiring founders, the prospect of building something from the ground up, with the potential for substantial financial rewards, is a powerful motivator.

The drive for innovation, the potential for disruption, access to funding, supportive regulations, operational agility, and personal ambition all contribute to the allure of entrepreneurship in the finance sector. As the market continues to evolve, the opportunities for new companies will likely expand, further incentivizing the creation of startups that can redefine the financial landscape.

However, it's important to recognize that the mere spark of an idea, no matter how compelling, does not always translate into action. Fear, false perceptions, or external influences can often hold individuals back from turning their entrepreneurial aspirations into reality. Many promising ideas may remain just that – ideas – unless the individual takes the time to thoughtfully examine and refine them.

Seeking advice from others can be immensely valuable, as it allows entrepreneurs to gain new perspectives and test the viability of their ideas. At the same time, it's crucial that the entrepreneur takes the time to thoroughly understand and shape the idea in their own mind before seeking external validation. After all, the initial idea is just the seed – it is through nurturing, iteration, and adaptation that it can grow into a thriving, full-fledged business.

The entrepreneurial journey is not without its challenges, but by embracing the inherent agility and adaptability of startups, as well as the personal drive to create something transformative, finance-focused entrepreneurs can position themselves to capitalize on the evolving market landscape and redefine the industry's future.

"Jump into the adventure" is a term used in startups to describe the mindset and approach required to succeed in entrepreneurship's fast-paced and uncertain world. It encapsulates the following concepts:

1. **Embrace Risk and Uncertainty:** Startups operate in a highly uncertain environment. Founders must be willing to take calculated risks and embrace the unknown.
2. **Be Agile and Adaptable:** Startups need to be able to pivot quickly and adapt to changing market conditions. *"Jumping into the adventure*" means being open to new ideas and adjusting course as needed.
3. **Have a Growth Mindset:** Startups are constantly evolving and growing. Founders must have a growth mindset and be willing to learn and improve continuously.
4. **Be Passionate and Driven:** Starting and running a startup requires immense passion and drive. The term "adventure" suggests that the journey will be challenging but also incredibly rewarding.
5. **Embrace Collaboration:** Startups often rely on collaboration with investors, mentors, and other stakeholders. "Jumping into the adventure" means being open to seeking help and building a strong support network.
6. **Be Bold and Fearless:** Success in startups requires boldness and the willingness to take risks. Founders must be fearless in pursuing their vision and overcoming obstacles.

Why is "*Jumping into the Adventure*" Important for Startups?

The allure of entrepreneurship in the finance sector lies in its ability to foster a dynamic culture of innovation and risk-taking – qualities that are essential for driving growth and disrupting the status quo. Unlike the more rigid structures of larger, established corporations, startups in the finance industry possess remarkable agility that allows them to navigate the uncertainty of rapidly evolving market conditions and make quick decisions in response to shifting consumer preferences and regulatory landscapes.

This operational flexibility is a key differentiator, empowering entrepreneurial teams to pivot and iterate their business models swiftly, seizing opportunities as they arise. Moreover, the prospect of building something transformative from the ground up attracts talented individuals who are excited by the challenge and the potential rewards of entrepreneurship. The sense of autonomy, coupled with the ability to directly impact the success of the business, serves as a powerful motivator, infusing the startup's culture with a palpable energy and purpose.

As entrepreneurs navigate the dynamic finance market, they are not only building their own ventures but also contributing to a broader ecosystem of innovation. By embracing a mindset of calculated risk-taking and a relentless drive to redefine the industry, these trailblazers are shaping the future of finance, pushing the boundaries of what's possible and inspiring others to follow in their footsteps.

In this environment, the rewards go beyond financial gain; they include the personal fulfillment of creating something impactful, the pride of fostering a talented and engaged team, and the satisfaction of disrupting an established industry. It is this unique blend of agility, innovation, and ambitious spirit that makes entrepreneurship in the finance sector an increasingly attractive path for those seeking to leave an indelible mark on the industry.

Examples of "Jumping into the Adventure" in Startups:

The spirit of entrepreneurship is often defined by a willingness to embrace uncertainty and leap into uncharted territories. In the dynamic world of startups, this "jump into the adventure" mentality manifests itself in a variety of ways, each representing the boundless creativity and unwavering determination that characterize the most successful ventures.

Consider the startup that decides to enter a new market despite the constraints of limited resources and the presence of formidable competition. Driven by a bold vision and a relentless pursuit of growth, these trailblazers are willing to venture into the unknown, confident in their ability to carve out a niche and disrupt the status quo.

Similarly, the founder who pivots the business model after receiving valuable feedback from early customers exemplifies the agility and adaptability that are hallmarks of the entrepreneurial spirit. Rather than clinging to a rigid plan, these savvy leaders are willing to course-correct, leveraging insights from the market to refine their offerings and better serve their target audience.

The team that embraces a transformative new technology, recognizing its potential to revolutionize the industry, also embodies the adventurous spirit of startups. These innovators are not content with the familiar; they are driven to push the boundaries of what's possible, driven by a relentless curiosity and a desire to shape the future.

Securing the necessary funding to fuel growth is another critical step in the startup journey, and those founders who are able to raise capital from investors who believe in their vision and execution capabilities are demonstrating their willingness to take calculated risks. They are not merely seeking the resources to sustain their operations; they are seeking partners who share their ambition and are willing to invest in their entrepreneurial dreams.

Finally, the founder who collaborates with experienced mentors and advisors, seeking out their wisdom and support, is further evidence of the entrepreneurial spirit in action. These leaders understand that they cannot go it alone, and they are humble enough to recognize the value of external guidance and the power of a strong support network.

Across these diverse examples, a common thread emerges the determination to embrace the unknown, pivot and adapt, and leverage every available resource in the pursuit of transformative change. It is this spirit of adventure that defines the most successful startups, propelling them forward and shaping the future of their respective industries.

Many of my friends and colleagues and I have founded one or more startups, each with its unique set of challenges and opportunities. These experiences have provided firsthand knowledge of the entrepreneurial process, from ideation to execution. And guess what? Not all of them work out.

So, what you will find in this text is that we don't all successfully execute the best ideas. Many of the people you read about never tell you about the failures, the bad decisions, the errors, the risks that were untaken, and the lost relationships and friends along the way.

But they had them, they will have them, and it is part of the adventure and the journey. I will, and others will in this text, talk about how hard it is and how gut-wrenching it is to have an idea come crashing to earth with you bearing all the weight.

Starting a new business or founding a startup can be an exciting but challenging endeavor. Here's a beginning guide to help you navigate the process: *(Just Jump in and get started)*

At the heart of this excitement lies the intersection of technological innovation, evolving consumer preferences, and a dynamic regulatory landscape. These elements combine to offer entrepreneurs a compelling opportunity to not only disrupt traditional financial models but also to create significant value and impact on a global scale.

Technological Innovation as a Catalyst

Technological innovation has become a driving force in the current financial landscape. The emergence of fintech has revolutionized the delivery of financial services, empowering new players to challenge established institutions with unparalleled efficiency and creativity. Technologies such as artificial intelligence, blockchain, and big data analytics are no longer the exclusive domain of large enterprises but are now accessible to startups and smaller organizations as well.

This democratization of technology has allowed new businesses to innovate at a rapid pace, introducing products and services that are more personalized, cost-effective, and user-friendly than those offered by traditional financial institutions. For entrepreneurs, the ability to leverage these technologies is not merely about gaining a competitive edge but rather about redefining the very nature of financial services.

AI-driven algorithms can now provide personalized investment advice; blockchain technology can ensure secure and transparent transactions and big data analytics can help predict market trends with remarkable accuracy. These advancements have enabled new organizations to operate with a level of sophistication that was unimaginable just a few years ago. This not only enhances their potential for financial success but also positions them as leaders in the ongoing transformation of the financial industry.

Evolving Consumer Preferences: A New Frontier

The shift in consumer preferences is another driving force behind the excitement of starting a new financial organization. Today's consumers are more informed, empowered, and demanding than ever before. They expect financial services to be accessible, transparent, and tailored to their individual needs. This shift is particularly pronounced among younger generations, who are digital natives and are more likely to adopt and trust new financial technologies. They seek out services that align with their values, such as sustainable investment options and are more open to experimenting with innovations like cryptocurrencies and peer-to-peer lending platforms.

For entrepreneurs, this change in consumer behavior presents a wealth of opportunities to develop products and services that resonate with modern consumers. By focusing on user-centric design and leveraging technology to deliver highly personalized experiences, new organizations can differentiate themselves in a crowded market. The ability to build strong, loyal customer relationships based on trust and mutual benefit is a powerful driver of success in today's finance market. Furthermore, as consumer expectations continue to evolve, the potential for continuous innovation keeps the entrepreneurial journey both challenging and rewarding.

The growing demand for personalized, tech-driven financial solutions has created an environment ripe with opportunities for innovative startups. Consumers, particularly younger generations, are eagerly seeking out services that cater to their changing needs and preferences. By understanding this shift in consumer behavior, entrepreneurs can develop products and services that effectively address the pain points of modern financial consumers.

At the heart of this opportunity lies the power of technology. New organizations can leverage cutting-edge tools like AI, blockchain, and big data analytics to deliver experiences that are tailored to individual users. This user-centric approach not only enhances customer satisfaction but also helps to build strong, loyal relationships based on trust and mutual benefit - a key driver of success in today's rapidly evolving finance market.

As consumer expectations continue to evolve, the entrepreneurial journey within the financial sector remains both challenging and rewarding. The potential for continuous innovation and disruption keeps the landscape dynamic, presenting a wealth of opportunities for those who can capitalize on the changing tides of consumer behavior and technological advancement.

Navigating the Regulatory Landscape

The regulatory landscape in the financial sector is constantly evolving, adding both complexity and excitement to the process of starting a new organization. While navigating regulations can be challenging, it also presents opportunities for innovation and differentiation. Regulatory bodies around the world are increasingly recognizing the need to adapt their frameworks to accommodate new technologies and business models. Initiatives such as regulatory sandboxes allow startups to test their products in a controlled environment, providing valuable feedback and reducing the risk associated with bringing new financial products to market.

For entrepreneurs, successfully navigating this regulatory landscape requires agility, creativity, and a deep understanding of both the legal environment and the broader market dynamics. Those who can effectively manage these challenges are not only more likely to achieve compliance but also to gain a competitive advantage. Being able to operate within the regulatory framework while still delivering innovative and valuable services to consumers is a key factor in building a sustainable and successful financial organization.

The dynamic nature of financial regulations presents both obstacles and openings for aspiring entrepreneurs. On one hand, the need to comply with a complex and ever-changing set of rules can add significant complexity to the process of launching a new venture. However, this same regulatory environment also creates opportunities for those who can navigate it with agility and foresight.

Regulatory bodies around the world are increasingly recognizing the need to adapt their frameworks to accommodate technological advancements and innovative business models. Initiatives like regulatory sandboxes provide a safe space for startups to test their products and services while also receiving valuable feedback and guidance from authorities. This not only helps to reduce the risk associated with bringing new financial solutions to market but also allows entrepreneurs to differentiate themselves by leveraging regulatory changes to their advantage.

Successful navigation of the financial regulatory landscape requires a deft combination of legal expertise, market acumen, and strategic thinking. Entrepreneurs who can effectively manage these challenges are not only more likely to achieve compliance but also to gain a competitive edge. By operating within the evolving regulatory framework while still delivering innovative and valuable services to consumers, these organizations position themselves for long-term sustainability and success in the rapidly transforming financial industry.

The Broader Impact: Beyond Financial Gain

While financial gain is undoubtedly a significant motivator for entrepreneurs, the excitement of starting a new organization in today's finance market goes beyond monetary success. The potential to make a meaningful impact on an industry that is central to the global economy is a powerful driving force. By disrupting traditional financial models, creating value through innovation, and addressing unmet needs in the market, entrepreneurs have the opportunity to contribute to broader societal and economic change.

This potential for impact is not just about creating profitable businesses; it's about driving progress and improving the lives of individuals and communities. Whether through expanding access to financial services, promoting financial literacy, or fostering economic inclusion, new organizations in the finance sector have the potential to make a significant positive difference. For many entrepreneurs, this sense of purpose and the opportunity to leave a lasting legacy is what makes the journey truly fulfilling.

For those with the vision and the willingness to embrace risk, the finance sector offers a rich tapestry of opportunities to disrupt traditional models, create value, and drive meaningful change. The journey of building a new financial organization is not just one of financial gain but also of personal and professional fulfillment, as entrepreneurs contribute to the ongoing transformation of one of the most vital sectors of the global economy.

The Benefits of Launching Your Business Today

The finance sector, traditionally dominated by large institutions, has experienced significant disruption in recent years, making it a fertile ground for innovative startups and new organizations. This essay explores the thrill and potential of launching a financial venture in today's dynamic market, considering the convergence of technology, changing consumer behavior, and the evolving regulatory landscape.

1. Changing Financial Landscape

One of the primary sources of excitement when starting a new organization in today's finance market is the rapidly changing landscape. The rise of fintech, or financial technology, has democratized access to financial services. What was once the exclusive domain of banks and financial institutions is now open to a broader range of players, from tech startups to non-traditional financial entities. This shift has created numerous opportunities for new entrants to challenge established players with innovative products and services.

For example, fintech companies have disrupted traditional banking by offering more accessible and user-friendly services, such as peer-to-peer lending platforms, digital wallets, and robo-advisors. These innovations not only provide consumers with more choices but also lower the barriers to entry for new organizations. Entrepreneurs can now leverage technology to offer financial services that are faster, cheaper, and more efficient than those provided by traditional institutions.

The selected text emphasizes the transformative impact of fintech on the finance industry. Fintech has democratized access to financial services, allowing a broader range of players, including tech startups and non-traditional financial entities, to enter the market. This shift has created numerous opportunities for new entrants to challenge established players with innovative products and services.

Examples of fintech innovations include peer-to-peer lending platforms, digital wallets, and robo-advisors, which provide consumers with more choices and lower the barriers to entry for new organizations. Entrepreneurs can leverage technology to offer financial services that are faster, cheaper, and more efficient than those provided by traditional institutions.

2. Leveraging Technology

Another aspect that fuels excitement is the role of technology in transforming the finance industry. Artificial intelligence (AI), blockchain, big data, and machine learning are revolutionizing how financial services are delivered. These technologies enable new organizations to develop products that were unimaginable a few years ago. For instance, AI-driven algorithms can provide personalized financial advice, while blockchain technology is reshaping everything from payment processing to identity verification.

The potential to harness these technologies is a major draw for entrepreneurs. Startups can innovate at a pace and scale that was previously impossible, allowing them to rapidly develop and deploy new solutions that address unmet needs in the market. Moreover, the widespread adoption of smartphones and the internet has made it easier than ever to reach a global audience, providing new organizations with the potential to scale quickly.

The selected text highlights the transformative impact of technology on the finance industry. Technologies like **artificial intelligence (AI)**, **blockchain**, **big data**, and **machine learning** are revolutionizing financial services by enabling the development of innovative products and solutions. For example, AI-driven algorithms can offer personalized financial advice, while blockchain technology is reshaping payment processing and identity verification.

These advancements are particularly exciting for entrepreneurs, as they allow startups to innovate rapidly and address unmet market needs. The widespread adoption of smartphones and the internet further facilitates reaching a global audience, enabling new organizations to scale quickly.

3. Responding to Changing Consumer Behavior

The shift in consumer behavior is another factor contributing to the excitement of starting a new organization in the finance market. Today's consumers are more tech-savvy, demand convenience, and expect personalized services. They are no longer satisfied with the one-size-fits-all approach that many traditional financial institutions offer. This change in consumer expectations presents a golden opportunity for new organizations to differentiate themselves by offering tailored solutions.

For example, millennials and Gen Z consumers are more likely to use mobile banking apps, invest in cryptocurrencies, and seek out sustainable investment options. New financial organizations can cater to these preferences by offering innovative products that resonate with these demographic groups. By understanding and anticipating consumer needs, startups can build strong, loyal customer bases.

4. Navigating the Regulatory Environment

Finally, while the evolving regulatory environment presents challenges, it also adds to the excitement of starting a new organization in the finance market. Regulations are adapting to keep pace with technological advancements, and this creates both opportunities and risks for new entrants.

Navigating this complex landscape requires agility, creativity, and a deep understanding of the market, which can be intellectually stimulating for entrepreneurs.

In conclusion, the excitement of starting a new organization in today's finance market is driven by the convergence of technological advancements, changing consumer behavior, and a dynamic regulatory environment. For those with a vision and the courage to innovate, the financial sector offers a landscape rich with opportunity, where new ideas can flourish and disrupt the status quo.

Idea Generation and Validation:

Start by identifying a business idea. Consider your interests, skills, and market needs. Validate your idea by conducting market research, seeking feedback, and assessing the viability of your business concept.

Now, the statements made in the prior paragraph are valid and noteworthy. But when it comes to ideas, I feel you don't always need to consider your interests and skills. We will go over the validation parts next. Let me give you an example.

When we started the algae business, we had no idea about algae. It was not an interest; it was not on our minds and certainly not in our skill set. We were looking at growing a plant for biofuels, a Jatropha Plant, in the desert, like in Mojave.

We researched the need for biofuels and felt it was a good business to investigate; by the way, we didn't know anything about biofuels either. As we were doing research, we were cautioned about the amount of water that would be necessary and that the land we were speculating on was not "wet" enough. We did not get discouraged, nor were we done researching. Then, one night, we were asked to attend a biofuel seminar where the president of a major oil company was going to speak on biofuels, so we went. It was in Palo Alto, California, the heart of the investment world that we knew at the time.

Well, there we sat listening to all the speakers talk, then at the end, the President guy took the podium. Out of his mouth was the statement that they, as a company, would be investing over 500 million dollars into the research of algae as a biofuel. We did the pivot before it was a thing, right then and there. Now, we had to become algae experts, not because we were. And we did just that.

So, my point is this: we were not skilled, interested, or even looking, but we were listening to what was being stated about the direction of the market and where investments may be available. We went on to engineer the largest close-looped photobioreactor in the world for carbon capture and storage, with the outcome being biofuels.

Keep an open mind, do your research, be ready to pivot, and be ready to jump at a moment's notice. It will be an adventure you will never regret.

Business Planning:

Creating a comprehensive business plan is a crucial step in launching a successful startup. This document serves as a roadmap for your business, outlining your strategy, operations, and financial projections. While the primary objective of a business plan may be to attract investors, it is essential to approach its development with a broader perspective.

The process of crafting a business plan should not be viewed solely as a means to secure funding. Rather, it should be an exercise in thoroughly understanding your business, its target market, value proposition, and operational realities. This deeper understanding will not only help you secure investment but also guide your decision-making and strategic planning as you navigate the challenges of building and growing your organization.

To ensure a business plan is a valuable tool for your startup, consider involving members of your team beyond the founders. Engaging a dedicated researcher or intern to handle the research and writing can free up your time to focus on the strategic aspects of the plan. This approach allows you to provide input and oversight while delegating the time-consuming tasks of data gathering and document formatting.

When deciding on the format of your business plan, weigh the pros and cons of a traditional paper-based document versus a digital, software-based approach. The former may be more familiar to some investors, while the latter offers greater flexibility and ease of updates. Ultimately, the choice should be driven by the preferences and expectations of your target audience, as well as the nature and complexity of your business.

Regardless of the format, the business plan should serve as a living, evolving document that reflects the changing realities of your startup. While the initial plan may be used to secure funding, it should not be discarded once your business is operational. Rather, it should be regularly updated to align with your actual objectives, operations, and market dynamics. This ongoing refinement will ensure the business plan remains a valuable tool for guiding your startup's growth and decision-making.

In summary, the creation of a business plan is a multifaceted exercise that extends beyond simply securing investment. By approaching it with a broader perspective, involving your team, and selecting the appropriate format, you can develop a plan that serves as a strategic roadmap for your startup's success, both in the short-term and long-term.

Paper Business Plan:

Tangibility

The tangible nature of a paper business plan can hold appeal for certain audiences, particularly those with backgrounds in more technical or analytical fields, such as accounting or science. The physicality of a printed document allows for easy review, note-taking, and sharing among multiple stakeholders. This can be advantageous in formal meetings or presentations, where a polished, well-organized physical plan can make a professional impression.

Accessibility and Flexibility

Moreover, the accessibility of a paper plan is a noteworthy consideration. Anyone can pick up and read a printed document without needing specialized devices or software, eliminating potential compatibility issues. For entrepreneurs who enjoy the process of physically writing and sketching out ideas, a paper-based plan can offer greater flexibility for handwritten notes and diagrams.

Evolving Investor Expectations

However, as the startup landscape has evolved, the value of the traditional paper business plan has diminished in the eyes of many investors and industry observers. The primary purpose of a business plan is to raise awareness and secure capital for your venture, and in today's fast-paced environment, there are often more engaging and technologically advanced ways to present your business model and growth strategy.

Digital Advantages

Digital, software-driven business plans offer a range of advantages that may better align with the expectations and preferences of modern investors. These platforms often provide greater flexibility for updates, real-time data integration, and interactive elements that can enhance the overall presentation experience. Furthermore, the environmental awareness surrounding the impact of paper usage has led some stakeholders to favor more sustainable, digital-first approaches.

Aligning with Your Audience and Goals

Ultimately, the choice between a paper-based or software-driven business plan should be driven by a holistic assessment of your target audience, the nature of your business, and the specific goals you aim to achieve through the planning process. By carefully considering the pros and cons of each format, you can ensure that your business plan serves as a valuable tool for guiding your startup's success, both in the short-term and long-term.

Software-Based Business Plan:

Dynamic Content: Digital software allows for dynamic and interactive content. You can include multimedia elements, links to relevant resources, and interactive charts that enhance the presentation of your business plan.

Collaboration: Collaborative tools in software platforms enable team members to work on the business plan simultaneously, facilitating real-time collaboration and updates. This is especially valuable for businesses with remote teams.

Version Control: Software-based plans often have version control features, making it easy to track changes, revert to previous versions, and maintain a comprehensive history of edits.

Integration: Many software platforms offer integrations with other business tools, allowing for seamless connectivity between your business plan and other aspects of your operations, such as financial software or project management tools.

Security: Digital platforms often have security measures in place, such as encryption and access controls, to protect sensitive business information.

Accessibility Anytime, Anywhere: Software-based business plans can be accessed from any device with an internet connection, providing flexibility for entrepreneurs who are constantly on the move.

Data Analysis: Digital plans can include data analytics tools, enabling you to embed dynamic charts and graphs that automatically update with real-time data.

Cost Efficiency: While some software solutions may come with a cost, they can be more cost-effective in the long run, especially considering the potential for collaboration, integration, and updates without the need for physical printing.

Hybrid Approach: In some cases, a hybrid approach might be suitable. You could create a digital business plan for dynamic and collaborative work and then produce a printed version for formal presentations or situations where a physical document is preferred.

Ultimately, the choice between paper and software depends on your specific needs, preferences, and the expectations of your audience. Consider the advantages of each format and how they align with your business goals and communication style.

Legal Structure and Registration:

Choose a legal structure for your business, such as a sole proprietorship, partnership, LLC, or corporation. Register your business with the appropriate government authorities and obtain any necessary licenses or permits.

You will find a myriad of advice and considerations in this area. While we are not legal advisors, we can tell you that this is an important phase and process of your business. But it can all be fixed later if necessary. So, spend some time but not a lot of time in this area of decision-making.

Choosing the right legal structure for your business is crucial and impacts various aspects, including liability, taxation, and management. I will not deliberate on the many legal structures in this text. It is sufficient to say that you will need to employ some legal counsel to fully understand your options from a tax as well as an administration point of view.

Consider the longevity and continuity of the business, especially if you plan to pass it on to future generations.

It's advisable to consult with legal and financial professionals for personalized advice based on your specific business goals and circumstances. Each legal structure has advantages and drawbacks, and the optimal choice depends on your business's unique characteristics.

Additionally, the place of incorporation, or formation, is important due to all of the tax ramifications in today's market, such as the tax difference between state and federal jurisdictions. However, do not spend a large amount of time on this decision; it can be adjusted in the future if necessary, such as if a partner(s) changes or the business grows in a different direction than what was originally expected.

Chapter 6: Procrastination

"The general who wins the battle makes many calculations in his temple before the battle is fought. The general who loses makes but few calculations beforehand."

-Sun Tzu, The Art of War

Let's start the adventure with an issue that is my Kryptonite: **procrastination**, delays due to overthinking, and roadblocks to the goal line. It all begins with the following:

"Shoulds," "coulds," and *"woulds"* are often associated with conditional statements or expressions of possibility, and they may or may not be delays in progress, depending on the context. Let's break down each term:

Shoulds:

"***Should***" is often used to express obligation, duty, or advisability. For example, saying *"I should complete this task"* implies a sense of responsibility or a recommended course of action. In some cases, the use of "*should*" might indicate a perceived delay if the action is not immediately taken. However, it can also be a way to prioritize tasks and plan actions.

Coulds:

"Could" is often used to express possibility or ability. For example, saying "*I could attend the meeting*" indicates that attending is a feasible option. The use of "*could*" doesn't inherently imply a delay; instead, it suggests a range of possibilities or choices.

Woulds:

"*Would*" is often used to express a hypothetical or conditional situation. For example, saying *"I would do it if..."* indicates a condition that needs to be met for the action to occur, like "*could*," the use of "*would*" doesn't necessarily imply a delay but rather introduces a condition or circumstance.

Whether these expressions contribute to delays in progress depends on how they are used and the context in which they are applied. In some cases, constant use of "Shoulds," "Coulds," and "Woulds" without decisive action may indeed lead to delays. However, these expressions can also be part of a thoughtful decision-making or planning process.

It's essential to be mindful of how these terms are used in communication and to recognize when they may be indicative of indecision or hesitation. In certain situations, replacing these conditional expressions with more direct and actionable statements may help in moving forward more efficiently.

Procrastination can have several negative impacts on businesses, affecting both individuals and the overall organization. The consequences of procrastination in a business context can be as varied as the businesses themselves. Procrastination often leads to missed deadlines. This can result in delayed projects, unmet client expectations, and a negative impact on the company's reputation.

As we look to create strategy and KPIs (Key Performance Indicators) for our team and business, missed deadlines create more than just a feeling of loss and concern but also a view of our leadership qualities and the overall direction. Sometimes, it is more important to revisit the timelines of our actions and plans and readjust them rather than miss deadlines.

Our observations about the negative consequences of procrastination and missed deadlines are spot on. Businesses must address these issues and implement strategies to mitigate the impact on both project outcomes and overall company reputation.

One of the key areas is to ensure that communication channels are open and transparent within the team. Encourage team members to communicate challenges and roadblocks that may affect deadlines. Foster a culture where team members feel comfortable discussing potential delays without fear of punishment. Not all communications are going to be to the acceptance of all the members of your team. It is in those instances that you can innovate and challenge the normal business ideas that are at the center of your company. Communication increases innovation and discourse around new ideas and ways of doing business.

When team members feel stuck or under-directed, they will fall into a position of procrastination due to lack of direction. It is important that we set realistic and achievable deadlines for projects. I have always found that managing tasks for employees with deadlines and timelines allows for more creativity in the completion of the task. Moreover, this way, the task is more likely to be completed with less oversight. The team members will also learn and have the freedom to create within the timeline, which is what you want long-term. Overly ambitious timelines can lead to stress and increased chances of missed deadlines and undesired results.

Consider involving team members in the timeline-setting process to get input on the feasibility of proposed deadlines. Implement regular check-ins to review project progress. This allows for early identification of potential delays and provides an opportunity for proactive adjustments.

Use project management tools and methodologies to track progress and identify areas that may need additional attention. I recommend that any tools you utilize be ubiquitous across all your organizations. This will allow for compatibility in cross-support, training, and reporting areas.

It is worth mentioning that not all your employees will be trained in the way you're expecting. In this case, it is essential to train them with respect and patience and give them time to develop advanced skills that align with your expectations. I recommend a Continuous Educational Program that might model similar industries and professional certification programs. By providing training and development opportunities to enhance the skills of team members, a well-equipped team is more likely to meet deadlines efficiently.

As you clearly define priorities and allocate resources effectively, make sure that you collaborate with your team and ask for input and recommendations. Remember, they are the ones ultimately responsible for the outcomes of the tasks assigned to them. Ensure that team members are aware of the importance of each task and how it contributes to the overall project goals.

Assess workloads regularly to prevent burnout and ensure that team members have the necessary resources to meet deadlines. Conduct post-project reviews to analyze what went well and what could be improved. Use this feedback to refine processes and strategies for future projects. Clearly communicate expectations regarding project deadlines, milestones, and individual responsibilities. Break down larger projects into smaller, manageable tasks to make the workload more digestible.

Encourage a mindset of continuous improvement, where the team is always seeking ways to optimize workflows and enhance efficiency. Help employees develop effective time management skills. This includes prioritizing tasks, breaking them into smaller, more manageable steps, and using tools or techniques to stay organized.

Acknowledge that unforeseen challenges may arise and build flexibility into project plans to accommodate unexpected issues. Foster an adaptable culture where your team is comfortable adjusting plans when necessary. Lead by example and demonstrate a commitment to deadlines. Show accountability for your own tasks and responsibilities. Provide clear expectations and hold your team members accountable for meeting deadlines.

By incorporating these principles into your strategy and KPIs, you can create a proactive and adaptive approach to managing deadlines, minimizing the negative impact on projects and the company's reputation.

Procrastination in the workplace:

When employees procrastinate, it can lead to decreased productivity as tasks take longer to complete. This inefficiency can hinder overall business operations and performance. In the end, we are reviewed by our internal and external clients based on the productivity that we can measure. So, as always, be transparent in your productivity measurements and honest with all the stakeholders. It may be hard at first, but it will pay off in the long run with more collaboration and opportunities for great team accomplishments.

These statements highlight the importance of addressing procrastination in the workplace and emphasize the significance of transparency and honesty in productivity measurements. Here are some additional thoughts and tips on dealing with procrastination and fostering a more productive work environment.

Understand the reasons behind procrastination. It could be due to a lack of motivation, unclear goals, fear of failure, or other personal and professional factors.

Acknowledge and reward employees for their accomplishments and productivity. Recognition can serve as positive reinforcement and help employees stay motivated and focused on tasks.

Allow for some flexibility in work schedules or offer remote work options. Flexibility can cater to individual preferences and workstyles, promoting a more conducive environment for productivity.

Maintain open lines of communication. Encourage employees to discuss their workload, deadlines, and any challenges they might be facing. Create a supportive environment where team members feel comfortable expressing concerns without fear of judgment. Recognize the importance of breaks for maintaining focus and creativity. Encourage short breaks throughout the day. Consider implementing policies that allow employees to take mental health days when needed.

Regularly ***assess the effectiveness of productivity strategies***. Be open to feedback and be willing to adjust approaches based on the evolving needs of the team and the organization.

By addressing procrastination and implementing strategies to enhance productivity, businesses can create a more efficient and collaborative work environment, leading to positive outcomes for both internal and external stakeholders.

Rushed work due to procrastination may result in lower-quality output. This can affect the quality of products, services, or deliverables, impacting customer satisfaction and loyalty. When we rush, we compromise the integrity and quality of our performance.

Every client looks for quality over time, and while we need to manage both, our focus should always be on quality.

This will produce long-term clients and greater success, and it will also help establish a positive reputation for your work.

Rushed work often leads to errors, oversights, and lack of attention to detail, which can be detrimental to the overall success of a project or business.

Quality is a key factor in building trust with clients. Delivering high-quality products or services not only meets their expectations but also exceeds them, leading to increased satisfaction. Satisfied clients are more likely to become repeat customers and may even recommend your business to others.

On the contrary, rushed and subpar work can result in dissatisfaction, complaints, and a tarnished reputation. Negative word-of-mouth spreads quickly, and it can be challenging to regain trust once it's lost. Clients may be forgiving of delays if the result is of high quality, but they are less likely to forgive poor-quality work delivered on time.

To ensure long-term success, it's crucial to prioritize quality in all aspects of your work. This may involve better time management, setting realistic deadlines, and avoiding the temptation to procrastinate. Investing time and effort into producing excellent work pays off in the form of satisfied clients, positive reviews, and a strong business reputation.

Procrastination can contribute to increased stress levels among employees as deadlines approach. This stress can have a cascading effect on morale, teamwork, and the mental well-being of employees. In the business world, we need to de-stress our workload, delegate when necessary, and allow others to accomplish the tasks we have given them for them to grow. You may be tempted to try to do everything yourself, but the best strategy is choosing your battles wisely.

Once you understand that you can't do everything yourself and learn to delegate your work efficiently, you will see that being an entrepreneur can become significantly easier.

Another obstacle to timely deliveries is procrastination. Procrastination is often linked to poor time management. When employees consistently delay tasks, it becomes challenging to allocate time effectively, leading to a cycle of uncompleted work.

With the creation of workplace environments that stretch all over the world, time management becomes a critical factor in production. The global workforce is a distinct advantage to most organizations. The ability to manage time allocations and production levels will be greatly dependent on your ability to delegate with confidence.

Remember, you have team members that you trust who were hired to help you, so let them do their job. Do not micromanage them regarding time; manage them regarding tasks assigned.

Procrastination can indeed be linked to poor time management, and this becomes particularly significant in the context of a globalized workforce. Effective time management is essential not only for individual productivity but also for the overall success of an organization, especially in a globalized setting.

If there are poor time management skills at the management level, it will trickle down to the workforce in the form of procrastination. If your employees see a pattern of poor time management, they, too, will procrastinate and miss important deadlines, slowing down the entire company's production.

Here are a few key aspects to consider in the context of time management in the workplace:

Different Time Zones: In a global workforce, teams may be spread across various time zones. Effective time management becomes crucial in such instances to ensure that tasks are completed efficiently and deadlines are met despite the challenges posed by different working hours.

Communication Challenges: With teams spread across the world, communication becomes a critical factor. Clear and timely communication is vital for coordinating tasks, sharing information, and addressing any issues that may arise.

Poor time management can lead to delays in communication, affecting collaboration and project timelines.

Task Prioritization: Employees need to prioritize tasks effectively, considering the urgency and importance of each assignment. Procrastination can lead to tasks piling up, making it difficult to meet deadlines and deliver quality work.

Technology and Tools: Utilizing technology and productivity tools becomes essential in a global work environment. This includes project management software, communication tools, and time-tracking applications. However, these tools are only effective if employees manage their time well and consistently use them. It is important to enforce punctuality from management positions, as your actions act as examples for your employees.

Cultural Awareness: Different cultures may have varying approaches to time and work. Understanding and respecting these cultural differences is crucial for effective collaboration.

Poor time management that leads to missed deadlines can strain relationships and hinder the success of cross-cultural teams.

Flexible Work Arrangements: With the rise of remote work and flexible schedules, employees need to manage their time responsibly. Procrastination can be more tempting when working outside a traditional office setting, making it even more critical for individuals to take control of their time.

Organizations can address these challenges by fostering a culture of effective time management, providing training on time management skills, and promoting open communication.

Encouraging a proactive and disciplined approach to work can help employees overcome procrastination and contribute to the success of a globally dispersed workforce.

Missed Opportunities: Procrastination can lead to missed opportunities for innovation, business development, or strategic planning. Delaying important decisions or actions may result in the loss of potential advantages in the market and missed deadlines, causing frustration among team members who may be relying on the completion of certain tasks to move forward. This can create a domino effect, impacting the overall progress of projects and contributing to a sense of stagnation.

When this becomes a recurring pattern, it may foster an environment where deadlines are not taken seriously, and accountability for timely delivery is eroded.

Procrastination can indeed have significant negative consequences, especially in professional and business contexts. In rapidly changing industries, delaying decisions or actions may mean losing out on a chance to be the first mover or losing the ability to capitalize on emerging trends. In competitive markets, hesitation or delay can result in a competitive disadvantage.

Competitors who are quicker to adapt, innovate, or implement strategic plans gain a stronger foothold in the market. Project delays can result in missed opportunities. For example, if a product launch is delayed, competitors may seize market opportunities, and the project may not achieve its full market potential.

Innovation often brings about new opportunities, whether it's entering new markets, forming strategic partnerships, or creating novel revenue streams. Procrastination can result in missed chances to capitalize on these opportunities, limiting the overall growth potential of a business.

Innovation Stagnation:

Procrastination can stifle innovation. In dynamic industries, staying ahead often requires continuous innovation. Delaying the development and implementation of new ideas can result in a company falling behind its more proactive counterparts.

Reputation Damage:

Consistent procrastination may harm a company's reputation. Stakeholders, including customers, investors, and partners, may lose confidence in a business that appears indecisive or slow to respond to challenges.

Persistent procrastination can erode trust within a team or with clients. Trust is essential for effective communication, and when team members or clients cannot rely on timely and high-quality deliverables, it can strain relationships and make communication more challenging.

Inefficiency in Communication:

Procrastination can result in a lack of proactive communication. Team members may not share progress updates or challenges in a timely manner, leading to a lack of transparency and making it difficult for others to adjust their plans accordingly.

To mitigate these challenges, it's important for individuals and teams to foster a culture of accountability, set realistic deadlines, and encourage open and transparent communication. Additionally, adopting time management strategies and addressing the root causes of procrastination can help improve overall productivity and communication within a team or with clients.

When tasks are delayed, resources such as time, money, and manpower may be wasted. Projects may require additional effort to catch up, resulting in increased costs and decreased profitability.

Delays in completing tasks within a project can have significant consequences, impacting various resources and overall project success. Here are some key aspects that can affect productivity as well as the success of any project:

Timelines: Delays can disrupt project schedules and timelines. This may affect the overall project completion date and potentially lead to missed deadlines. It can also affect subsequent tasks that depend on the completion of delayed activities.

Money: The saying *Time is money* perfectly describes the impact of procrastination on a business. Time is closely tied to costs in project management. Delays can lead to increased costs due to extended project durations.

Additional labor costs, overhead expenses, and penalties for missing contractual deadlines can contribute to financial strain for a business.

Manpower: Project teams are often organized based on specific timelines and task dependencies. Delays may require the reallocation of resources, leading to overburdened teams or the need to bring in additional personnel. This can impact team morale, productivity, and overall project cohesion. Overworked employees are not able to work to their full potential, and this results in subpar work, which affects the company's reputation.

Effort and Productivity: Catching up on delayed tasks often requires extra effort and resources. Team members may need to work overtime or under pressure, potentially leading to burnout and decreased productivity. Quality is also compromised when tasks are rushed to meet deadlines.

Client Satisfaction: Delays can negatively affect client satisfaction, especially if there are contractual obligations or client expectations regarding project timelines. This may harm the reputation of the project team or the organization.

Risk Accumulation: Delays can increase the exposure to various risks. External factors, such as changes in market conditions or technology, may pose new challenges during an extended project timeline.

Procrastination may lead to a situation where urgent and hasty decisions are made, which can carry higher risks than a carefully planned and timely implementation.

To mitigate these risks, project managers often implement strategies such as effective planning, risk management, regular monitoring, and contingency planning. Timely communication with stakeholders is also crucial to managing expectations and proactively addressing issues.

Procrastination can negatively impact employee engagement and morale. Employees may feel frustrated or demotivated if they perceive a lack of progress or see their efforts hindered by procrastination within the organization, thus impacting team morale. When tasks are repeatedly delayed, team members may become frustrated or disheartened, contributing to a culture where individuals feel less motivated to hold themselves or others accountable.

To foster a culture of accountability, it's important for individuals and teams to address procrastination head-on. This may involve implementing effective time management strategies, setting realistic deadlines, and promoting open communication about challenges and progress. Additionally, leadership plays a crucial role in cultivating a culture of accountability by setting clear expectations, providing support, and addressing procrastination when it arises.

To address these issues, organizations should focus on promoting a proactive and organized work culture. This includes setting clear expectations, providing the necessary resources, and fostering a supportive environment where employees feel empowered to meet their responsibilities.

When tasks are put off until the last minute, employees may feel increased stress and pressure to meet deadlines.

This can negatively impact their mental well-being and lead to burnout, further diminishing overall morale.

Procrastination can create a culture of non-accountability, where individuals or teams may not take responsibility for their actions or inactions. This lack of accountability can erode trust within the team and decrease morale. When individuals or teams consistently delay tasks or fail to meet deadlines due to procrastination, it can create a culture where accountability is compromised.

Continuous procrastination can result in decreased productivity as tasks take longer to complete than initially planned. This inefficiency can be demotivating for employees who want to see tangible results for their efforts. Employees may perceive procrastination as a sign of inefficiency within the organization. This perception can lead to frustration, as team members may feel that their time and efforts are not being utilized effectively.

Procrastination can lead to a blame-shifting mentality. When faced with the consequences of delayed tasks, team members may start pointing fingers at each other or external factors. This can create a culture where individuals avoid taking responsibility for their own actions. Companies that are slow to adapt may develop a reputation for being behind the times. This perception can be damaging, affecting customer trust, investor confidence, and partnerships with other businesses.

Procrastination can significantly impede the timely implementation of new ideas or innovations, and this delay can have several negative consequences. Delaying the implementation of new ideas can erode the innovative culture within an organization. Over time, employees may become demotivated, and the company might struggle to attract top talent, both of which are crucial for sustained innovation. In rapidly evolving business environments, delaying necessary changes can result in a loss of competitiveness.

In rapidly evolving industries, staying competitive often relies on being at the forefront of innovation. Procrastination can result in missed opportunities to adopt new technologies or business practices, putting a company at a disadvantage compared to more agile competitors.

Consumer preferences and market trends can change rapidly. Procrastinating on implementing necessary changes might lead to a loss of relevance, as customers may shift their preferences toward businesses that offer more up-to-date products or services.

To counteract the negative effects of procrastination, organizations need to foster a culture of agility, encourage proactive decision-making, and prioritize ongoing innovation. This involves staying informed about industry trends, being open to change, and implementing a strategic approach to adapt to the evolving business landscape.

Businesses can promote a proactive and goal-oriented culture, provide time management training, encourage effective communication, and set realistic deadlines. Individual responsibility, effective leadership, and a focus on organizational efficiency are crucial in addressing the negative consequences of procrastination in a business setting.

Conclusion:

It is human nature to put off what we don't like or understand. This chapter goes into detail about procrastination, discussing thoroughly that your entire organization will suffer if a culture of procrastination is allowed to grow and mature in your organization.

I experienced this firsthand, which cost me dearly. That is why I am writing this book as a precaution to any entrepreneur who slips off their A-game. I want this story to be your wake-up call that business owners don't get a day off. We always have to be present for our work, both mentally and physically.

My partner and I were in a very controversial business to many in the energy and carbon industry: *algae for carbon capture and storage.* Two things that we did not procrastinate on were what led to us becoming one of the most sought-after companies in the region.

Firstly, we didn't procrastinate when figuring out how to engineer a reactor to create algae. We decided to construct a model that turned into the largest reactor of its kind, right in my backyard. Had we been waiting and wasted any time on rethinking our decision, we would never have been able to create the largest design in operation.

We started to build a desktop model, then decided not to doubt ourselves and create the best we could possibly create, so we did just that. We were able to finish it just in time to become industry leaders in a huge marketplace.

We did research and design reviews and took care of many other aspects of the operation and design. We delegated, involved, educated our team, set timelines, engaged outside help, and even made a few mistakes, but we kept at it and never doubted our business acumen, which led to our inevitable success.

The second thing I will forever be grateful for was that early on, we decided that due to an upcoming election, we needed to influence the new administration's next funding cycle. So, we engaged a lobbyist, went to Washington, and did some lobbying. With the help of a top-level law firm, we were able to change the law before it was enacted to the tune of about 1.5 billion dollars.

Had we procrastinated, none of that would have happened, and our budding business would have gone up in flames due to new regulations.

Whenever I procrastinate, it goes down badly.

There was a time when I decided to start an energy company that would focus on tariff energy contracts with the utility providers in my state.

It was a great plan; all was going great. We had secured several hundred contracts in less than 90 days, and things were looking good. We had a great team consisting of several dozen employees. We had even garnered a small investment to get started, and everything was good—that is, until we started to get too big too fast, and I was advised to slow down. But in my excitement about future prospects, I paid them no mind, and I did not listen to the advice.

I put off some hard decisions due to my excitement and lack of focus. I did not train my employees well enough for such situations and let them loose without clear direction. I handed over a key management position to a person that I had not trained enough, placing them in a position of ultimate failure.

All of these things combined, the future of the company looked bleak. Despite all of that, we were ignoring the inevitable storm, knowing we had a record-breaking company doing what no other had ever done in the utility space. We were full of ourselves, and that was for certain.

Well, I took on a few other tasks and was advised to shut some portions of the company down to save the rest, but I delayed making a decision. I delayed the opportunity to save what we created, and in that delay, we lost everything. **I lost everything**, professionally and personally.

Procrastination can really hold you and your business back. I've experienced the bad side of it firsthand and know the success you can achieve when you beat procrastination.

On the one hand, I've seen how putting things off can be disastrous. When I delayed making important decisions for my energy company, it ended up costing me everything -

professionally and personally. I let the excitement and lack of focus cloud my judgment, and it all fell apart because of my procrastination.

But I've also seen the incredible power of taking action and not procrastinating. With my algae reactor project, we just dove in and built the largest one in the world. And with that lobbying effort in Washington, we were able to secure a ton of funding before the window closed. If we had procrastinated, none of that would have happened.

I know from experience—both good and bad—the impact that procrastination can have. It's human nature to want to put things off; I get that. But you can't let it hold you back.

My advice? Don't procrastinate. If you need to slow down and plan things out, that's fine. But don't let your ideas and opportunities sit and gather dust. When you're ready, just go for it.

The world is waiting for you to make your move. Will you let procrastination be your downfall? Or will you harness that bias for action and propel your business to new heights?

The choice is yours. Stop waiting and start doing. Your success is on the line.

Chapter 7: Team Building

"Water shapes its course according to the nature of the ground over which it flows; the soldier works out his victory in relation to the foe whom he is facing."

-Sun Tzu, The Art of War

Building a Team:

When trying to build a team, make sure to recruit members with the skills and expertise needed to support your business. This may include co-founders, employees, advisors, or contractors. A strong team is essential for the success of your startup. It is the only reason and the driving force behind the success of your venture. A team is fundable, and the idea is not so much. A great team can create a winner, and a great team can sustain winning; an idea on its own cannot. The reason for this topic being the start of this chapter is that you just need a team, and understanding that from the start is essential.

Building a strong and effective team is essential for the success of any business. When we look at a team, we start to think about the positions everyone should play and the objectives of each section and player, but we fail to look at the real value a team member can play in our success. We tend to focus on what the rest of the world thinks that position should be categorized as the skill set, the degree, the associations, and the overall "skill" and not the person. The person needs to have passion, insight, and determination. This startup life is not for the weak of the heart. We have found great people who were smart, quick, intelligent, and driven from areas of the world and business that had nothing to do with where they found success in our organizations. As a startup, you need thinkers and doers and leaders, not degrees and social status that make you feel you are blessed to have them. You need people like you.

The success of any startup is intrinsically tied to the quality, skills, and cohesion of the team behind it. While ideas are often seen as the seeds of innovation, they are inert without the proper team to cultivate and bring them to fruition. A strong, capable team is not just an asset but the cornerstone of any successful venture. This essay explores the importance of building the right team for your startup, highlighting why a team is fundable and sustainable while an idea alone is not. We will also discuss how to identify the necessary skills and expertise required, the types of team members to consider, and strategies for assembling this team.

The Importance of a Strong Team

1. The Team is the Driving Force

A brilliant idea is the foundation of a startup, but without a capable team to execute it, the idea remains merely a concept. The team is the driving force behind the startup's journey from ideation to execution, scaling, and, ultimately, success. They bring the idea to life, making decisions, solving problems, and continuously innovating to adapt to market demands.

For instance, consider how Google, Apple, or Amazon became industry giants. It wasn't just the ideas of search engines, personal computers, or online retail that made them successful. It was the teams of skilled, dedicated individuals who worked tirelessly to refine these concepts, build scalable businesses, and navigate the challenges of growth and competition. A well-rounded team provides the necessary balance of creativity, technical expertise, business acumen, and leadership needed to turn an idea into a successful enterprise.

2. The Fundability of a Team

When it comes to securing investment, venture capitalists and investors often prioritize the quality of the team over the idea itself. This is because ideas are fluid; they can evolve, adapt, or pivot in response to market feedback. A strong, experienced team, however, is more likely to successfully navigate these changes and drive the startup toward success.

Investors understand that a great team can take a mediocre idea and turn it into a successful business, whereas a weak team might fail even with a groundbreaking idea. This is why the team is often seen as a more critical factor in securing funding than the idea itself. The presence of a cohesive, skilled team instills confidence in investors that the startup has the resilience and capability to overcome challenges and achieve long-term success.

3. Sustainability Through Team Dynamics

A great team not only creates a winning startup but also sustains its success over time. Startups face a myriad of challenges, from market competition to operational hurdles and financial constraints. A strong team with complementary skills and a shared vision can weather these storms, continuously innovate, and keep the startup on a growth trajectory.

The sustainability of a startup is directly linked to the strength of its team. The collective expertise, problem-solving abilities, and collaborative dynamics of a team are what enable a startup to maintain momentum and thrive in a competitive environment. In contrast, an idea alone, no matter how innovative, lacks the capacity to sustain itself without the right team behind it.

Identifying the Necessary Skills and Expertise

1. Core Competencies

To build a successful startup, it's essential to identify the core competencies required for your business. These competencies typically fall into three broad categories: technical, operational, and strategic.

Technical Skills: These are the specialized skills needed to develop the product or service your startup offers. For a tech startup, this might include software development, data science, or engineering. For a manufacturing startup, it might involve expertise in product design, supply chain management, and quality control.

Operational Skills: These skills are necessary to manage the day-to-day activities of the startup. This includes financial management, human resources, sales, marketing, and customer service. Operational expertise ensures that the startup runs smoothly and efficiently, allowing the technical team to focus on product development.

Strategic Skills: Strategic skills involve high-level decision-making, business development, and long-term planning. These skills are typically possessed by the founders or senior executives who set the direction of the startup and make critical decisions that affect its future.

2. Complementary Skill Sets

A successful team is one where the skills and expertise of its members complement each other. This means that each team member brings unique strengths to the table, filling gaps in the team's overall skill set. For example, a team might consist of a visionary CEO with strategic foresight, a technical co-founder with deep expertise in product development, a marketing expert who understands customer acquisition, and a financial officer who ensures fiscal responsibility.

Complementary skill sets are crucial because they allow the team to cover all aspects of the business, from ideation to execution, marketing, and scaling. This diversity in skills also fosters innovation, as team members with different perspectives can collaborate to find creative solutions to problems.

3. Cultural Fit and Shared Vision

While technical skills and expertise are critical, cultural fit and shared vision are equally important when assembling a team. A team that shares the same values, goals, and vision for the startup is more likely to work well together and remain committed to the startup's success, even during challenging times.

Cultural fit ensures that team members can collaborate effectively, communicate openly, and support each other. A shared vision keeps the team aligned and focused on the long-term goals of the startup, reducing the risk of conflicts and ensuring that everyone is working toward the same objectives.

Types of Team Members to Consider

1. Co-Founders

Co-founders are the backbone of any startup. They are typically involved from the very beginning and share the responsibility of shaping the startup's direction, culture, and vision. When selecting co-founders, it's important to choose individuals who not only bring complementary skills but also share your passion and commitment to the startup.

Technical Co-Founder: A technical co-founder is responsible for developing the product or service. This person should have deep technical expertise and the ability to lead a development team. In tech startups, the technical co-founder is often the CTO *(Chief Technology Officer).*

Business Co-Founder: A business co-founder handles the operational and strategic aspects of the startup. This person should have experience in business development, marketing, sales, and finance. In many startups, the business co-founder assumes the role of CEO (Chief Executive Officer).

Domain Expert: In some cases, it may be beneficial to have a co-founder who is a domain expert in the industry you are entering. This person brings valuable insights, industry connections, and credibility to the startup.

2. **Early Employees**

The first few employees you hire will play a significant role in shaping the culture and success of your startup. These individuals should be highly skilled, adaptable, and aligned with your startup's vision. Early employees often wear multiple hats, taking on various roles as the startup evolves.

Engineers and Developers: In tech startups, engineers and developers are often the first hires after the co-founders. They are responsible for building and refining the product, making them critical to the startup's success.

Product Managers: Product managers bridge the gap between the technical team and the business team. They ensure that the product meets market needs and aligns with the startup's overall strategy.

Sales and Marketing Professionals: Early sales and marketing hires are responsible for customer acquisition and brand building. They should have experience in go-to-market strategies, customer relationship management, and growth hacking.

Customer Support: As your startup begins to acquire customers, it's important to have a customer support team in place. These employees ensure customer satisfaction and retention by addressing issues and providing assistance.

3. **Advisors and Mentors**

Advisors and mentors bring valuable experience, knowledge, and networks to your startup. While they may not be involved in the day-to-day operations, their guidance can be instrumental in helping you navigate challenges and make informed decisions.

Industry Advisors: Industry advisors are experts in your startup's industry. They provide insights into market trends, regulatory requirements, and industry best practices.

Business Advisors: Business advisors have experience in scaling startups, fundraising, and business strategy. They can help you refine your business model, pitch to investors, and plan for growth.

Technical Advisors: Technical advisors have deep expertise in the technology your startup is developing. They can provide guidance on product development, technical challenges, and innovation.

4. Contractors and Freelancers

In the early stages of a startup, you may not have the resources to hire full-time employees for every role. Contractors and freelancers can provide the skills and expertise you need on a temporary or project basis. This allows you to access specialized skills without the long-term commitment of hiring full-time employees.

Designers: Freelance designers can help with branding, user interface (UI) design, and user experience (UX) design. Their work is critical in creating a visually appealing and user-friendly product.

Content Creators: Content creators, such as writers, videographers, and social media managers, can help build your startup's online presence and engage with your target audience.

Consultants: Consultants bring specialized knowledge in areas such as legal, finance, and human resources. They can help you navigate complex issues without the need for full-time staff.

Strategies for Assembling Your Team

1. Networking and Referrals

One of the most effective ways to find team members is through networking and referrals. Reach out to your professional network, attend industry events, and participate in startup communities to connect with potential co-founders, employees, and advisors. Referrals from trusted contacts can lead to high-quality candidates who are a good fit for your startup.

2. Recruiting Platforms and Job Boards

Recruiting platforms and job boards are valuable tools for finding talent. Platforms like LinkedIn, AngelList, and Glassdoor allow you to post job openings, search for candidates, and review resumes.

Here are **steps to help you assemble a team** with the skills and expertise needed to support your business:

(remember skills can be trained, thinking not so much, and wisdom is key as well.)

1. Identify Required Skills:

Clearly define the skills and expertise necessary for the success of your business. Consider both technical skills and soft skills relevant to your industry and the specific roles within your team.

When I refer to required skills, keep in mind that I did not say required passion or desire; I said Skills. This means that with the right person, you can train the skills and the task management necessary for a position to be successful based on skills application, not personal drive and desire. Do not limit your criteria based only on skills but also on the aptitude to acquire and apply the necessary skills.

2. Create Job Descriptions:

Develop detailed job descriptions for each role within your team. Clearly outline responsibilities, qualifications, and the skills required for success in each position.

When you get started, you will not fully understand or be able to process actual job descriptions. So, do not look to use this as a justification to not move forward. You will come across individuals that you can just place a tag on a position, but you know they have great potential and value. Move forward with them and find a position as you grow.

You will know that certain areas need an outline and description. That description will change over time, and the first person, as a startup, that you place in a position will more than likely not be in the same spot one year later. It is good to have that perspective because one year later, you will have several staff members who know several areas of the company, so your knowledge base will be multiplied.

3. Determine Team Structure:

Decide on the organizational structure of your team, including the hierarchy and reporting relationships. Consider whether a flat or hierarchical structure is most suitable for your business.

Start with a proposed organizational chart in any form that works for you. One that we have settled on is a model called Spherical Economy; we created the term and the model in our business designs based on the description of ***Holarchy***. In business terms, holacracy is a specific organizational structure and management philosophy that aims to distribute authority and decision-making throughout an organization. The term "holacracy" is derived from the words "holon" and "hierarchy." A holon is a self-contained unit that is simultaneously a part of a larger system (similar to a cell within a body). Holacracy seeks to create a flexible and adaptive organizational structure that allows for both autonomy and collaboration.

In a Holarctic organization, traditional hierarchical structures with top-down management are replaced by a system of self-organizing teams or circles. These circles operate with defined roles, responsibilities, and accountabilities, and they have the authority to make decisions related to their domain. Decision-making is often decentralized, and there is an emphasis on continuous improvement and adaptability.

4. Recruitment Strategy:

Develop a recruitment strategy to attract qualified candidates. This may include posting job listings on relevant platforms, networking, and utilizing recruitment agencies.

Recruiting Strategies for Startups

Recruiting the right talent is crucial for the success of startups. Here are some **effective recruiting strategies for startups**:

Define Your Company Culture: Clearly articulate your company's values, mission, and culture. This will help attract candidates who align with your startup's vision and are likely to thrive in your work environment. These statements and vision will help frame your path forward; they will change over time and possibly pivot in a direction that you didn't see coming due to markets, finance, trends and/or decisions made in industry positions.

Create a Compelling Employer Brand: Develop a strong employer brand by showcasing your startup's unique selling points, such as the innovative work you're doing, opportunities for career growth, and the positive aspects of your workplace culture. Use social media, your website, and other platforms to communicate this brand.

As your brand is created and or thought about, I suggest that you engage some outside reviews of what you are developing. A perspective from others outside of your organization will prove to be an asset in brand creation. Those who give you insight do not have to be brand professionals; remember your future audience, that is, the people that you should have brand conversations with.

Leverage Your Network: Tap into your personal and professional networks for potential candidates. Referrals from trusted sources can lead to high-quality hires. Encourage your current team to refer candidates and consider implementing a referral program. A referral program can be anything from cash to a free ride at the rodeo; be creative. The more creative you are, the more unique your Employer Brand will be, and others will seek you out, making your task much easier.

Your network includes every person on the team. That network may not be entirely in your field of endeavor, but they know people who want a change and have ambitions that would or could serve your organization well.

Utilize Online Job Platforms: Post your job openings on popular job boards, industry-specific websites, and social media platforms. This can help you reach a wider audience and attract candidates actively seeking new opportunities. The use of boards can be effective, but it can also use cash flow, which you cannot afford to use. So, be selective and do your diligence on the organizations you choose. They, too, will be viewed as part of your brand and organizational strategies from the outside looking in, so be selective.

Participate in Industry Events: Attend conferences, meetups, and other industry events to network with potential candidates. These events provide an opportunity for direct interaction and can help you identify individuals who are passionate about your industry.

The process of networking in your industry is key to many successful actions in the present and the future. I also recommend that you go to events in your area that have nothing to do with your industry. There, you may find those who have skills and ambition in organizational areas of your business, such as sales and administration, while you network with other industries.

Offer Competitive Compensation: While startups may not always be able to match the salaries offered by larger companies, it’s essential to provide competitive compensation packages. Consider other benefits such as flexible work schedules, stock options, and professional development opportunities.

These can be items such as discount programs at local retailers, legal clubs for personal issues, summer camps for the kids, art classes for spouses, and many other benefits that other organizations do not offer but can be a value add for your team.

Highlight Learning and Growth Opportunities: Emphasize the learning and career growth opportunities your startup offers. Many talented individuals are attracted to roles where they can develop new skills and take on increasing responsibilities.

Considering this, our organization offers continued education credits and offers in many areas of business and personal growth that are fully paid for by the organization. These credits can be placed toward advancement, rewards, project deployments, and bonuses.

Streamline the Hiring Process: Startups often need to move quickly in the hiring process to secure top talent before larger companies do. Streamline your hiring process to avoid unnecessary delays and communicate clearly with candidates about the expected timeline.

Consider more than one hiring manager in each interview, and get it done quickly and with compassion for the interviewee's time as much as your own. Speed in the hiring process can be accomplished when a process is in place. Maybe work with an outside firm to help with the heavy lifting of the Human Resources process, such as policy, onboarding, compliance, and handbook administration.

When you are decisive in the hiring process, it will blend over to the work environment, and the expectation to act and make decisions will be a company style versus an anomaly.

Emphasize the Impact of the Role: Communicate how each role contributes to the overall success of the startup. Talented individuals are often motivated by the opportunity to make a significant impact and see the results of their work.

The impact of every team member needs to be highlighted. In this part of team building, I feel it is best to introduce other team members that a person might be working with and get to know each other for a moment. Talk about how, in a startup, everyone matters; everyone is a key part of the puzzle. Also, let everyone know that with time, there will be many opportunities to advance and grow into other areas of the business. This will reduce the thought of boredom over time in any one position.

Implement Internship Programs: Consider offering internship programs that can serve as a pipeline for future full-time hires. Internships allow both the employer and the intern to assess the fitness for a more permanent role.

In most areas, interns are valued and respected workers. They need to be compensated accordingly, by ethics and by law in most areas. I feel that we sometimes only look at the young college-age person as an intern, and with that, we are missing a very valued workforce. For those who are in between industries and careers, as well as those who have retired or have time on their hands, An intern can be anyone that you feel adds value and can grow to be an asset for the organization.

Be Transparent: Be open and transparent about the challenges and opportunities within your startup.

Transparency builds trust and helps candidates make informed decisions about joining your team.

All businesses have issues, and in some cases, we don't want anyone to know, at least those coming in from another organization. However, there is strength in the complete transparency of an organization in all matters that are relevant. You may find that that person has knowledge or connections that can help. It is a way of asking for involvement in the growth of the organization, not just a task-oriented person who cannot think outside of any given task. Be transparent; you will find it greatly rewarding, and you will find help where you thought there was none.

Embrace Remote Work: Consider offering remote work options, especially if your startup is not located in a major tech hub. This expands your talent pool and allows you to attract candidates from diverse geographical locations.

The great thing about technology is that it can be utilized from any place on the planet and beyond. The bad thing about technology is that it can be utilized from any place on the planet and beyond.

Using technology to add to your resources does not take away from it; it can be a tool for remote working, education, and collaboration. With today's technical abilities, you have a real need to have everyone working in a cubicle or bullpen in your cozy office. If you hire the right people, and some will not be, that is the game, but most will be; let them use the skills you hired them for and go remote. It will save you lots of money on rent and utilities.

Remember that assembling a high-performing team is an ongoing process. Regularly assess the team's performance, provide opportunities for growth, and remain attentive to the evolving needs of your business.

There are many tools, software, and others in today's marketplace that can help with many of these steps and the ongoing maintenance of the team. Continuing education and support are what keep a team engaged and thinking. The process should be a cultural creation that includes learning every day, even in areas that may not be organizationally specific. Let me give you an example:

I had a guy who worked for a computer company, who, at the time, was a great guy and a hard worker. He was intelligent and did his job well. Upper management came by one day and said we needed to make some shift changes. I was a new manager and really had no idea what I was doing, so I did what the upper management said to do. I moved people around in order to fulfill someone else's desires.

The results were mixed. Some did not care, others were adapting, and some were not happy. At the start, I identified that this person was one of the not-so-happy types. As I watched him begin to underperform, miss work, be angry, and just become a pain to all involved, I decided to ask him what the issue really was. As it turned out, he had a passion for baking, and he was enrolled in classes that he could not attend, although he had already paid for them. And he was thinking of quitting and was angry over the entire operation.

So, I worked with him and readjusted his scheduled work times, endorsed his efforts publicly to the team, and encouraged him to bring his baked goods to work. He became the best team member I had for several years, and he advanced in the organization as well. He was getting stimulation and education that made him happy, and he was a great team member. Although baking had nothing to do with his current occupation, it just made him happy. And after all, that is the goal here in team building**: happy teams create success for all.**

Chapter 8: Trends, Setbacks, Challenges, and Market Dynamics

"In the midst of chaos, there is also opportunity."

-Sun Tzu

Staying ahead of industry trends is crucial for professionals and businesses to remain competitive and adaptable. Here are some strategies to help you stay informed about the latest developments in your industry:

Continuous Learning:

Cultivate a mindset of continuous learning. Regularly attend workshops, webinars, conferences, and industry events to acquire new knowledge and skills. Online platforms, industry associations, and educational institutions often offer relevant courses. The process of learning extends beyond the classroom and webinars. Routinely participate in sessions that are not directly related to your core business strategy. This allows you to discover new trends and insights that may impact your business in unexpected ways. Treat every day as an opportunity to learn something new.

Industry Publications and Journals:

Subscribe to industry-specific publications, journals, and magazines. These sources often provide in-depth analysis, case studies, and insights into emerging trends and best practices. Maintain an online database of relevant information that you can easily access and leverage for research and other growth initiatives. Explore the authors and contributors of these publications and connect with them to build your professional network.

Networking:

Build and maintain a strong professional network within your industry. Attend networking events, join professional associations, and engage with peers, colleagues, and thought leaders. Networking can provide valuable firsthand information about industry trends. While networking may feel uncomfortable for some, it's a crucial skill to develop. If you feel uneasy in a networking situation, acknowledge it aloud to the people you're talking to. This can help reduce the stress and facilitate more meaningful relationship-building.

Social Media Monitoring:

Remain active on social media platforms to follow industry influencers, organizations, and relevant hashtags. Platforms like LinkedIn, Twitter, and industry-specific forums can be excellent sources of real-time information and discussions. While new media platforms emerge constantly, avoid spending excessive time on them unless it is directly tied to your business. Consider hiring a dedicated team member to manage your social media presence, as it can play a major role in most businesses. Maintain a professional, focused, and non-controversial approach on these platforms.

Industry Reports and Market Research:

Regularly review industry reports and market research studies. Organizations, research firms, and industry associations often publish comprehensive insights into market trends, challenges, and opportunities.

Competitor Analysis:

Monitor your competitors to understand their strategies, product launches, and market positioning. Analyzing competitor behavior can help you identify emerging trends and potential areas for innovation.

Join Online Communities:

Participate in online forums, discussion groups, or community platforms related to your industry. Engaging with industry peers in these spaces can provide valuable insights and perspectives.

Podcasts and Webinars:

Listen to industry-related podcasts and participate in webinars. These platforms often feature experts and thought leaders discussing the latest trends, challenges, and innovations. Consider creating your own podcast as a means to advertise and engage with others in your field.

Cross-Industry Insights:

Look beyond your specific industry to gain insights from related or adjacent sectors. Cross-industry trends can sometimes have implications for your own field.

Mentorship and Advisory Relationships:

Seek mentorship from experienced professionals in your industry or related fields. Having mentors and advisory relationships can provide guidance and insights into emerging trends.

Internal Knowledge Sharing:

Encourage knowledge sharing within your organization. Create forums or regular meetings where team members can share insights and updates about industry trends they've come across.

Monitor Regulatory Changes:

Stay informed about any regulatory changes or policy shifts that may impact your industry. Government agencies and regulatory bodies often announce changes that can influence industry dynamics.

Invest in Professional Development:

Invest in your professional development by attending training sessions, workshops, and certifications. Building your expertise can give you a deeper understanding of industry trends.

Technology Adoption:

Keep an eye on technological advancements and innovations relevant to your industry. Embracing new technologies can often be a key component of staying ahead in today's rapidly evolving business landscape.

Remember, staying ahead of industry trends is an ongoing process, and a combination of these strategies tailored to your specific industry and role can be most effective. Regularly reassess and adjust your approach to ensure that you stay well-informed and adaptable.

Gaining valuable insights into market dynamics, customer behavior, and competitive landscapes is crucial for building a successful business. Understanding these aspects can inform various aspects of your operations and strategy.

Informed Decision-Making:

Armed with insights into market dynamics, you're better positioned to make informed decisions. This could include product development, pricing strategies, and marketing efforts tailored to the specific conditions of your industry. Leveraging data-driven insights allows you to make more strategic choices that are aligned with the realities of your market.

Customer-Centric Approach:

Recognizing the importance of customer behavior implies a customer-centric mindset. By understanding your customers' needs, preferences, and pain points, you can tailor your products and services to meet their expectations, fostering customer satisfaction and loyalty. This customer-centricity helps you develop offerings that truly resonate with your target audience, strengthening your brand and relationship with your clientele.

Adaptability to Market Changes:

A deep understanding of market dynamics allows you to adapt to changes effectively. Markets are inherently dynamic, and being attuned to shifts in trends, consumer demands, or competitive landscapes helps you stay agile and responsive. This adaptability enables you to pivot your strategies as needed, ensuring your business remains relevant and competitive in the face of evolving market conditions.

Competitive Advantage:

Competitor analysis provides insights into the strengths and weaknesses of other players in your industry. Leveraging this information, you can identify opportunities to differentiate your business, offering unique value propositions and gaining a competitive advantage. By understanding your competitors' strategies, product offerings, and market positioning, you can develop a clear and distinctive value proposition that sets your business apart.

Targeted Marketing Strategies:

With insights into customer behavior, you can tailor your marketing strategies more effectively. This might involve personalized messaging, targeted advertising, or specific promotions that resonate with your target audience. Utilizing customer data and behavioral insights allows you to craft marketing initiatives that are laser-focused on your ideal clients, improving the efficiency and effectiveness of your marketing efforts.

Innovation Opportunities:

Understanding market dynamics often reveals opportunities for innovation. Whether it's in product design, distribution channels, or business models, being aware of market trends can help you identify areas where innovation can set you apart. Identifying unmet needs, emerging technologies, or evolving customer preferences can inspire innovative solutions that disrupt the status quo and position your business as an industry leader.

Risk Mitigation:

Comprehensive market research helps identify potential risks and challenges. This proactive approach allows you to implement risk mitigation strategies, reducing the impact of uncertainties on your business. By anticipating and preparing for potential market disruptions, regulatory changes, or competitive threats, you can position your organization to weather unexpected storms more effectively.

Customer Retention Strategies:

Customer-centric strategies go beyond acquiring new customers. They are also involved in implementing effective customer retention strategies. Satisfied and loyal customers contribute to the long-term success of your business. By understanding what drives customer loyalty and satisfaction, you can develop initiatives that keep your existing clientele engaged and committed to your brand.

Strategic Planning:

Armed with market insights, you can develop more effective strategic plans. These plans can guide your business in the short and long term, aligning your goals with the realities of the market. By grounding your strategy in a deep understanding of your industry, you can ensure your objectives and initiatives are well-positioned for success.

Resource Optimization:

Knowing your market and customers allows for more efficient resource allocation. You can focus on initiatives and areas that are most likely to yield positive results, optimizing both time and budget. This data-driven approach to resource management helps you maximize the impact of your investments and avoid wasting valuable resources on endeavors that may not align with market demands.

Measuring and Monitoring Performance:

Market insights provide benchmarks for measuring your business's performance. Regularly monitoring key performance indicators against industry trends helps you assess your progress and make data-driven adjustments. This continuous evaluation and refinement of your strategies ensures your business remains responsive and adaptable to evolving market conditions.

Embracing setbacks and failures as valuable learning opportunities is a hallmark of a resilient and adaptive mindset. These challenges can become stepping stones for personal and professional growth, fostering qualities that are essential for long-term success.

Resilience Building:

Overcoming setbacks fosters resilience. Resilient individuals are better equipped to handle adversity, bounce back from failures, and maintain a positive attitude in the face of challenges. This resilience becomes a valuable asset, allowing you to persevere through difficult times and emerge stronger.

Adaptability and Flexibility:

Setbacks necessitate adaptability. Those who embrace change and are flexible in their approach can navigate uncertainties more effectively. Adaptable individuals are often better positioned to thrive in dynamic and evolving environments, as they can quickly pivot their strategies and tactics in response to new circumstances.

Problem-Solving Skills:

Failures provide opportunities to enhance problem-solving skills. Each setback is a puzzle to be solved, encouraging individuals to think critically, analyze situations, and develop creative solutions. This ability to effectively address challenges and find innovative ways forward is a valuable skill set in any business context.

Learning and Growth:

Failures are rich sources of learning. Each experience, whether positive or negative, contributes to personal and professional growth. Reflecting on setbacks helps identify areas for improvement and development, fueling a continuous cycle of learning and self-improvement.

Iterative Progress:

Embracing failures as part of a continuous learning process allows for iterative progress. Each setback becomes a feedback loop, leading to adjustments, improvements, and an evolving approach to challenges. This mindset of constant refinement and optimization enables you to consistently enhance your capabilities and strategies over time.

By prioritizing market research, a customer-centric approach, and a positive perspective on setbacks, you can position your business for sustained success and growth. Continuous learning, adaptability, and a growth mindset will be key drivers in navigating the dynamic and ever-evolving business landscape.

Chapter 9: A Reflection on the Collision of Finance and Startups

Plan for what is difficult while it is easy, and do what is great while it is small.

-Sun Tzu

In modern capitalism, the intersection of finance and startups has become a critical juncture—a point where dreams meet dollars, where innovation collides with valuation, and where the ambitions of entrepreneurs converge with the often unforgiving logic of the market. This collision, which has been the subject of exploration throughout **The Broken Line,** is not merely a meeting of two worlds but rather a dynamic and evolving battlefield where ideas are tested, refined, and sometimes destroyed by the forces of capital.

Final Summation: The Anatomy of Finance for Startups

In the realm of entrepreneurship, financial stability is the bedrock upon which successful startups are built. A comprehensive understanding of the financial landscape is paramount for founders seeking to navigate the complexities of funding, investment, and growth. This final summation aims to provide a comprehensive overview of the financial elements essential for startups, from seed funding to eventual exits.

The Genesis of Growth

In the initial stage of startup financing, seed funding provides the necessary capital to establish the business, develop a prototype, and test the viability of the concept. Sources of seed funding include friends and family, angel investors, and venture capitalists. The valuation of the startup at this early stage is typically low, as the business is still in its formative phase.

Scaling the Heights

As the startup gains traction and expands its operations, Series A funding becomes necessary to accelerate growth.

This round of financing typically involves venture capitalists and institutional investors. The valuation of the startup increases significantly compared to seed funding, reflecting the progress made and the potential for scalability.

Securing Growth Capital

Series B funding is sought to further expand the startup's market share and solidify its position in the industry. This round often involves a diverse mix of investors, including venture capitalists, growth equity funds, and strategic partners. The valuation of the startup continues to increase as its revenue and customer base grow.

Funding and Beyond Fueling Expansion

Depending on the nature of the business and its growth trajectory, startups may seek additional rounds of funding, such as Series C, D, and beyond. These rounds are typically led by venture capitalists and private equity firms. The valuation of the startup reaches its peak during these later stages, reflecting its maturity and established market presence.

Exit Strategies: Realizing Value

The ultimate goal of any startup is to achieve a successful exit. There are multiple exit strategies available, including:

- **Initial Public Offering (IPO):** The startup goes public by selling shares of its stock on the stock market. This strategy provides access to a large pool of investors and can result in a substantial windfall for founders and early investors.

- **Acquisition:** Another startup or a larger corporation acquires the startup. This option provides a quick and straightforward path to liquidity but may limit the upside potential for founders.
- **Strategic Partnership:** The startup enters into a strategic alliance with another company, sharing resources and expertise to drive growth. This strategy can provide access to new markets and accelerate development, but it also involves giving up some control.

Financial Management: A Foundation for Success

Beyond fundraising, effective financial management is crucial for startups. This includes:

Budgeting and Cash Flow Forecasting: Establishing a clear budget and accurately forecasting cash flow is essential for ensuring financial stability and making informed decisions.

Profitability Analysis: Tracking key financial metrics, such as gross margin, operating expenses, and net profit, helps startups identify areas for improvement and ensure long-term profitability.

Financial Reporting and Compliance: Adhering to relevant financial reporting standards and compliance requirements is essential for maintaining transparency and building investor trust.

Empowering Founders

Navigating the financial complexities of startups is a challenging but ultimately rewarding endeavor. By understanding the fundamentals of funding, investment, and financial management, founders can position their ventures for success. This final summation has provided a comprehensive overview of the financial elements that entrepreneurs must master to build sustainable, high-growth startups.

Navigating the financial complexities of startups is indeed a challenging but ultimately rewarding endeavor. The process demands a deep understanding of various financial elements, including funding, investment, and financial management. These components are the cornerstones upon which successful, high-growth startups are built. Entrepreneurs who master these elements can position their ventures for long-term success, mitigating risks and capitalizing on opportunities as they arise. This essay provides a comprehensive overview of the financial strategies that entrepreneurs must employ to build and sustain a thriving startup.

The startup ecosystem is inherently complex, characterized by uncertainty, rapid change, and high stakes. Entrepreneurs operate in an environment where the margin for error is thin, and financial missteps can lead to failure.

However, those who navigate this complexity with a clear understanding of financial fundamentals often find themselves in a stronger position to succeed. At the core of this ecosystem are several critical factors, including the ability to secure funding, attract investment, and manage finances effectively.

Crafting a Strong Business Plan

A strong business plan is the foundation of any successful fundraising effort. It outlines the startup's vision, mission, and strategy, providing investors with a clear understanding of the business's goals and how it plans to achieve them. The business plan should include detailed financial projections, market analysis, competitive landscape, and a roadmap for growth. It should also address potential risks and how the startup plans to mitigate them. A well-crafted business plan not only attracts investors but also serves as a guiding document for the startup's growth and development.

Demonstrating Market Potential

Investors are particularly interested in startups that operate in large or rapidly growing markets. Demonstrating market potential involves conducting thorough market research to understand the size, growth rate, and key trends within the industry. Entrepreneurs must be able to articulate how their product or service addresses a significant market need and how they plan to capture a substantial share of the market. This requires a clear value proposition, a well-defined target audience, and a deep understanding of the competitive landscape.

Building a Strong Team

A strong team is often one of the most critical factors in a startup's success. Investors look for teams that have the skills, experience, and passion necessary to execute the business plan and drive the startup to success. This includes not only the founders but also key hires in areas such as product development, marketing, and finance. Entrepreneurs must be able to demonstrate that they have assembled a team capable of overcoming the challenges that lie ahead and delivering on the startup's potential.

Creating a Scalable Business Model

Scalability is a key consideration for investors, as it determines the startup's ability to grow rapidly and generate significant returns. A scalable business model is one that can be expanded without a corresponding increase in costs, allowing the startup to achieve economies of scale. This often involves leveraging technology, streamlining operations, and developing partnerships that enable the business to reach a larger audience or enter new markets. Entrepreneurs must be able to show that their business model is not only viable but also scalable, with the potential to generate substantial revenue and profit.

Managing Investor Relations

Once the investment is secured, managing investor relations becomes a critical aspect of the startup's financial strategy. This involves regular communication with investors, providing updates on the startup's progress, and being transparent about challenges and setbacks. Building and maintaining strong relationships with investors can lead to additional funding opportunities, valuable advice, and support during difficult times. Entrepreneurs must strike a balance between meeting investor expectations and retaining the flexibility to make decisions that are in the best interest of the startup.

Financial Management: The Backbone of Startup Success

Effective financial management is the backbone of any successful startup. It involves not only managing cash flow and budgeting but also making strategic decisions about where to allocate resources, how to price products or services, and when to raise additional capital. Financial management is a dynamic process that requires constant monitoring, analysis, and adjustment.

Cash Flow Management: Staying Afloat

Cash flow management is one of the most critical aspects of financial management for startups. Cash flow refers to the movement of money in and out of the business, and managing it effectively is essential to ensuring that the startup can meet its financial obligations. Positive cash flow indicates that the business is generating more money than it is spending, while negative cash flow can lead to financial difficulties and, ultimately, failure. Entrepreneurs must be diligent in monitoring cash flow, forecasting future needs, and taking proactive steps to address cash flow issues before they become critical.

Budgeting and Forecasting: Planning for the Future

Budgeting and forecasting are essential tools for financial planning in startups. A budget outlines the startup's expected income and expenses over a specific period, serving as a roadmap for managing finances and making informed decisions. Forecasting, on the other hand, involves predicting future financial performance based on historical data, market trends, and other factors. Both budgeting and forecasting require careful analysis and regular updates to reflect changes in the business environment. By maintaining a realistic budget and accurate forecasts, entrepreneurs can better manage their resources, plan for growth, and avoid financial pitfalls.

Pricing Strategy: Balancing Value and Profitability

Pricing strategy is a critical component of a startup's financial management, as it directly impacts revenue and profitability. Setting the right price for a product or service requires a deep understanding of the target market, the perceived value of the offering, and the competitive landscape. Entrepreneurs must strike a balance between pricing that attracts customers and pricing that ensures profitability. This may involve experimenting with different pricing models, such as subscription-based pricing, tiered pricing, or freemium models. It is also important to regularly review and adjust pricing strategies based on market conditions, customer feedback, and cost structures.

Raising Additional Capital: Timing and Strategy

At some point, most startups will need to raise additional capital to fund growth, expand operations, or overcome financial challenges. Knowing when and how to raise capital is a critical aspect of financial management. Entrepreneurs must carefully consider the timing of fundraising efforts, as raising capital too early or too late can have significant consequences. They must also choose the right type of funding, whether it be equity financing, debt financing, or alternative sources.

As we reach the conclusion of this journey, it is essential to reflect on the themes, lessons, and paradoxes that have emerged from the stories and analyses that populate this book. The world of startups, with its boundless energy, relentless optimism, and fearless pursuit of the new, stands in stark contrast to the world of finance, which, despite its own appetite for risk, is ultimately driven by the need for return, security, and control. The collision between these two forces is neither a simple clash nor a harmonious fusion; it is a complex interplay that shapes the trajectories of companies, markets, and even entire industries.

One of the central themes that has emerged is the fragility of the startup ecosystem when subjected to the pressures of financial markets. Startups, by their nature, are built on uncertainty. They thrive on disruption, seeking to carve out new spaces in the market or to redefine existing ones. However, the very essence of what makes a startup successful—its ability to innovate and take risks—also makes it vulnerable. When these young companies are thrust into the financial arena, they are often required to conform to metrics and expectations that may not align with their developmental stage or long-term vision.

The influence of venture capital, private equity, and public markets can be both a blessing and a curse for startups. On the one hand, access to capital is crucial for growth, enabling startups to scale their operations, attract talent, and expand into new markets. On the other hand, the demands of investors can lead to a focus on short-term gains over long-term sustainability, forcing companies to make decisions that may be detrimental in the long run. The pressure to achieve rapid growth, often at the expense of profitability, can lead to a *"grow or die"* mentality that has seen many promising startups burn out before they have had a chance to fully realize their potential.

This tension is further exacerbated by the cultural differences between the world of finance and the world of startups. While both are driven by a desire for success, their definitions of success can be fundamentally different. For many in the startup world, success is measured not just in financial terms but in the impact they have on the world—the problems they solve, the industries they disrupt, and the lives they improve. In contrast, the financial world is often more focused on measurable returns on the bottom line. This difference in perspective can lead to a misalignment of goals and expectations, creating friction that can hinder the growth and sustainability of even the most promising ventures.

Another critical theme explored in The Broken Line is the role of technology in reshaping the financial landscape and its implications for startups. The rise of fintech, blockchain, and artificial intelligence has opened up new avenues for innovation and disruption, challenging traditional financial institutions and creating new opportunities for startups. However, this technological revolution also presents significant risks. The rapid pace of technological change can make it difficult for startups to keep up, while the increasing complexity of financial systems can lead to unintended consequences, such as the creation of new forms of risk and instability.

Moreover, the globalization of finance has added another layer of complexity to the startup ecosystem. In a world where capital flows freely across borders, startups are no longer confined to local markets—they must navigate a global financial landscape that is influenced by a myriad of factors, from interest rates and currency fluctuations to geopolitical events and regulatory changes. This global dimension of finance adds both opportunities and challenges for startups as they seek to compete on an international stage while managing the risks associated with global financial markets.

Yet, despite these challenges, the collision of finance and startups also presents immense opportunities. The ability of startups to innovate and disrupt, combined with the resources and expertise of the financial world, has the potential to drive significant economic and social change. This symbiotic relationship, when managed effectively, can lead to the creation of new industries, the transformation of existing ones, and the development of solutions to some of the world's most pressing problems.

However, to fully realize this potential, both startups and the financial sector must learn to navigate the broken line that separates them. This requires a deeper understanding of each other's goals, challenges, and constraints. Startups must recognize the importance of financial discipline, while investors and financial institutions must appreciate the unique needs and timelines of early-stage companies. Both sides must be willing to engage in a dialogue that goes beyond the numbers, focusing on the long-term vision and impact rather than just short-term returns.

The broken line between finance and startups also reflects a broader societal issue—the tension between innovation and control, between creativity and regulation, between the pursuit of profit and the need for sustainability. As we move forward, it is essential that we find ways to balance these competing forces and create an environment where startups can thrive while also contributing to the broader good. This will require not only changes in how we think about finance and entrepreneurship but also in how we structure our economies, our markets, and our societies.

In conclusion, the collision of finance and startups is not just a story of conflict but also one of possibility. It is a story of how two seemingly disparate worlds can come together to create something greater than the sum of their parts. It is a story of how, despite the challenges and tensions, there is the potential for a new kind of capitalism—one that is more innovative, more inclusive, and more sustainable.

The road ahead will not be easy, and there will undoubtedly be more collisions and more broken lines. But if we can learn from the past and adapt to the changing landscape, there is no limit to what can be achieved. The key will be to embrace the uncertainty, to navigate the broken lines with creativity and resilience, and to forge a new path that balances the needs of both finance and innovation.

Ultimately, the collision of finance and startups is not just about the clash of two industries but about the collision of ideas, values, and visions for the future. It is about the struggle to reconcile the drive for innovation with the need for stability, the pursuit of growth with the importance of sustainability, and the desire for success with the responsibility to contribute to the common good. As we move forward, it will be essential to keep these tensions in mind, to navigate the broken line with care and thoughtfulness, and to strive for a future where the collision of finance and startups leads not to destruction but to creation, transformation, and progress.

Appendix of Terms

All men can see these tactics whereby I conquer, but what none can see is the strategy out of which victory is evolved.

-Sun Tzu, The Art of War

Investing in startups involves a unique set of terms and concepts. Not all are listed here, so if we missed a few, it is not due to the lack of clarity but maybe due to the length of terminology that is part of the startup lexicon. Not all are fully understood, and as such, may lead to misdirection. All these terms should be reviewed as they apply to your organization and the industry you work within. Some may have a better definition from your point of view, and that is good; we are looking to break a few molds.

Here are the top investment terms commonly used in the startup world:

A Culture of Innovation: Startups often cultivate cultures of innovation, creativity, and experimentation. This can be an attractive work environment for individuals who thrive on innovation.

Accelerator: A program that provides startups with mentoring, resources, and funding in exchange for equity, often culminating in a demo day.

Access to Capital: Investing facilitates the allocation of capital to businesses, supporting economic growth and job creation.

Accounts payable: The money a company owes to vendors/suppliers for inventory/services received but not yet paid off.

Accounts receivable: The money owed to a company resulting from providing goods/services to customers on credit.

Acqui-hire: An acquisition primarily motivated by the desire to hire a startup's talented team.

Actionable Takeaways: After discussions, distill the insights into actionable takeaways that can directly inform your strategic decisions and business plans.

Adapt to Investor Preferences: Some investors may have specific preferences for how they receive updates. Be flexible and accommodate their preferences whenever possible.

Advisory Board: Consider involving investors in an advisory board capacity. Their ongoing input can be invaluable to your decision-making process.

Advocacy for policy changes and lobbying for supportive frameworks

Alignment of Interests: Ensure that your investors' interests align with your strategic goals. If they have specific conditions or expectations, address them early to avoid conflicts later.

Alignment with the UN Sustainable Development Goals (SDGs): Many impact investors use the United Nations Sustainable Development Goals as a framework to guide their investments. These 17 global goals address critical challenges such as poverty, climate change, gender equality, and more.

Alternative Finance: Alternative finance refers to financial channels and instruments that exist outside of traditional banking and financial institutions. It encompasses a wide range of non-traditional methods of raising capital, financing projects, or facilitating financial transactions.

Alternative finance has gained prominence with the advent of technology and the rise of online platforms, allowing for new and innovative ways to connect borrowers with lenders or investors. Some examples of alternative finance include:

Angel Investing: Investment in startups and early-stage companies by individuals or groups outside the traditional banking sector.

Angel Investor: A high-net-worth individual who provides early-stage capital to startups in exchange for equity. Angels also often provide advice and contacts.

Ask for Their Insights: Encourage your investors to share their thoughts on your competitors. Ask for their observations, opinions, and any relevant data or anecdotes they may have.

Ask Open-Ended Questions: Encourage investors to share their views on market trends, industry shifts, and emerging opportunities. Ask open-ended questions that invite thoughtful responses.

Assess Compatibility: When you connect with potential mentors, assess whether there is compatibility in terms of values, vision, and communication style. A strong personal connection can enhance the mentorship relationship.

Balance sheet: A financial statement showing assets, liabilities, and equity at a specific point in time to demonstrate a company's net worth.

Bank Loans: These can include small business loans, SBA loans, microloans, equipment financing loans, credit lines, and factoring funding via a bank. Government grants may subsidize some bank loans.

Barriers to Entry: Ask for their assessment of barriers to entry for new competitors. What makes it difficult for others to enter your space?

Board Involvement: If you have a board of directors or advisory board, involve your investors in these discussions. Their participation can provide valuable input into strategic decisions.

Bootstrapping: Building and growing a startup without external funding, relying on revenue generated by the business.

Build Genuine Relationships: Focus on building genuine relationships with the individuals you are introduced to. Don't view them solely as a means to an end but as potential long-term collaborators.

Burn Rate: The rate at which a company is spending its financing before generating positive cash flow. Calculates how long the company can continue operating with its current funding, often expressed as a monthly or yearly expense.

Cap Table (Capitalization Table): A document showing the ownership structure of a company, including the shares owned by founders, investors, and employees.

Capital expenditure (CapEx): Funds used to acquire, upgrade, or maintain fixed assets like property, buildings, technology, etc.

Cash flow statement: Records the amounts of cash coming in and out of the business over a period of time. Indicates if there are more cash inflows/outflows and sources/uses.

Challenges and Solutions: Be transparent about the challenges and setbacks your startup has faced. Equally important, share the strategies and solutions you're implementing to overcome these challenges.

Clear Communication: Effective communication is key to a successful mentorship. Establish clear expectations, boundaries, and objectives from the outset.

Cofounder: An individual who collaborates with others to establish and build a startup company.

Collaboration: Impact investors often work closely with investees, providing not only financial capital but also strategic guidance and networks to help them achieve their social and environmental objectives.

Commitment: Understand that mentorship is a two-way commitment. Both you and your mentor should be committed to investing time, effort, and energy into the relationship.

Communication Plan: Outline how you plan to communicate progress and updates to your investors.

Regular updates are essential for maintaining alignment and trust.

Community Development Finance: Funding initiatives aimed at supporting local economic development and community projects.

Community-focused: Funding sources can include impact investors, community development financial institutions (CDFIs), or grants from foundations. Some startups may explore community development finance initiatives that align with their mission and goals.

Competitive Analysis: Seek their input on competitive analysis. They can provide an outside perspective on your strengths and weaknesses compared to competitors.

Competitive Positioning: Explain how your startup intends to differentiate itself in the market. Highlight your unique selling propositions and competitive advantages.

Competitive Threats: Explore potential threats from new entrants or disruptive players in the market. Investors may have insights into emerging competition.

Complex Market Dynamics: Commodities are influenced by various factors such as weather conditions, geopolitical events, and global economic trends. Understanding these dynamics requires in-depth research and expertise in commodity markets.

Content Clarity: Ensure that your updates are clear, concise, and organized. Use headings, bullet points, and visuals if necessary to make the information easily digestible.

Continual Feedback: Encourage your investors to provide feedback on the introductions they make. This feedback loop can help refine your networking strategy.

Continuous Learning: Approach mentorship as an ongoing learning experience. Be open to new perspectives and be willing to adapt and grow based on the insights you gain.

Continuous Monitoring: Discuss how you can continually monitor the competitive landscape. Investors can help you stay updated on industry changes and evolving competition.

Convertible Note: A debt instrument that can convert into equity at a later date, often used in early-stage financing.

Core Values: Define the core values and principles that guide your startup's culture and decision-making. Values provide a framework for ethical and strategic choices.

Cross-Validation: When possible, cross-validate the insights you receive from multiple investors and other industry sources. This helps ensure the reliability of the information.

Crowdfunding: Platforms that allow individuals or businesses to raise funds from a large number of people. Crowdfunding - Raising small amounts of money from a large number of people, typically via the Internet and social media. Popular platforms include Kickstarter, Indiegogo, and GoFundMe. This taps into the "crowd" to fund ideas.

Cryptocurrency and Blockchain-Based Finance: Digital currencies and blockchain technology that enable decentralized and secure financial transactions.

Customer Acquisition: Seek advice on customer acquisition strategies, marketing channels, and customer retention techniques.

Customer Insights: Inquire about their understanding of customer needs and preferences within your target market. Their insights can inform product development and marketing strategies.

Customer Insights: Inquire if they have insights into customer preferences and perceptions of your startup and its competitors. Understanding customer behavior can be a competitive edge.

Define Your Goals: Clarify your goals and objectives for the mentorship. What do you hope to achieve with the help of a mentor? Having clear goals will guide your search.

Discuss Competitive Landscape: Seek their perspective on the competitive landscape. Who are the key players? What strategies are competitors employing? Are there gaps or opportunities in the market?

Distribution Channels: Discuss the distribution channels competitors use and how your distribution strategy compares. Are there opportunities to optimize your distribution?

Diverse Perspectives: If you have multiple investors, leverage their diverse perspectives. Different investors may bring unique insights to the table.

Diverse Sectors: Impact investing spans various sectors, including but not limited to clean energy, affordable housing, healthcare, education, sustainable agriculture, and access to finance for underprivileged communities.

Diversification: Commodities have historically exhibited a low correlation with traditional asset classes such as stocks and bonds. By including commodities in a portfolio, investors can achieve greater diversification, potentially reducing overall portfolio risk. Commodities can act as a hedge against inflation and provide returns that are not closely tied to economic cycles.

Documentation: Document your objectives and vision in a clear, concise, and easily accessible format. This ensures that all stakeholders, including team members and investors, have a common understanding.

Documentation: Keep records of the insights and advice provided by your investors. These insights can serve as a valuable resource for future strategic planning.

Due Diligence: Conduct due diligence on your investors as well. Understand their track record and whether their expertise matches your business needs.

Due Diligence: The process of investigating and evaluating a startup's financials, operations, and legal matters before making an investment.

Emerging Technologies: Explore their views on emerging technologies that could disrupt or enhance your industry. Understanding technology trends can inform your product development.

Emotional Support: The entrepreneurial journey can be challenging and stressful. Mentors can provide emotional support, helping you navigate the ups and downs of startup life.

Engage in Strategic Discussions: Initiate strategic discussions with your investors that are specifically focused on market dynamics. Frame these discussions as opportunities to benefit from their experience and expertise.

Entrepreneurial Vision: Entrepreneurs often have a vision for a product, service, or technology that they are passionate about. Starting a new organization allows them to pursue this vision and turn their ideas into reality.

Equity: Ownership shares in a company, typically given to investors in exchange for capital.

stablish a Schedule: Set a regular schedule for updates. This could be monthly, quarterly, or according to milestones or significant events. Consistency is key.

Ethical Concerns: Some investors have ethical concerns about the industries or companies they may inadvertently support through their investments, such as those involved in controversial activities.

Existing Analysis: Present your current competitive analysis, if you have one. This can serve as a starting point for discussion and help investors understand your current views.

Exit Multiple: A measure of how much a startup's exit value exceeds the total investment made in the company.

Exit Strategy: Discuss potential exit strategies with investors. They can advise on when and how to consider acquisition offers, IPOs, or other exit options. If relevant, describe your startup's potential exit strategies, such as acquisition or initial public offering (IPO). This helps investors understand your long-term vision.

Feedback and Accountability: Mentors offer constructive feedback on your ideas, strategies, and plans. They hold you accountable for your goals and help you track progress.

Feedback Loop: Encourage feedback from your investors regarding your objectives and vision. Their insights can provide valuable perspectives and help refine your strategic direction.

Feedback Loop: Encourage honest feedback from your investors. They should feel comfortable sharing their concerns or suggestions, even if they differ from your current strategy.

Feedback Loop: Encourage your investors to share ongoing market insights with you. Markets are dynamic, so maintaining an open channel of communication is essential.

Feedback Loop: Establish a feedback loop to ensure the mentorship is on track and meeting your goals. Regularly communicate your progress and any challenges you're facing.

Feedback Solicitation: Encourage feedback from your investors. Ask for their insights, suggestions, or concerns regarding your startup's progress and strategy.

Financial forecasting - The process of making predictions about a firm's financial future based on assumptions about business activity such as sales, expenses, cash flows, etc.

Financial Management: Investors may have expertise in financial management and can provide guidance on budgeting, financial planning, and cash flow management.

Financial Potential: Successful startups have the potential for significant financial rewards. Founders and early employees may benefit from equity ownership and the potential for high returns.

Financial Projections: Provide financial projections that align with your objectives. These should include revenue forecasts, expense budgets, and key financial metrics.

Financial Returns: While impact investors prioritize making a positive difference, they still expect financial returns on their investments. This sets impact investing apart from traditional philanthropy, which typically involves charitable donations without the expectation of financial gain.

Financial Updates: Include financial updates such as revenue, expenses, and cash flow statements. Compare actual financial performance to projections, explaining any variances.

Flexibility: Startup founders have the flexibility to shape their own work environments, cultures, and work-life balances. This can be appealing to those who value autonomy.

Follow Up Promptly: When your investors make introductions, follow up promptly and professionally. Express your appreciation for the introduction and explain your interest in connecting.

Formal or Informal: Mentorship relationships can be formal, with structured meetings and defined objectives, or informal, based on casual interactions and ongoing advice.

Fractional banking facilitates the flow of money in the economy, supporting economic activity. However, it also poses risks, such as the potential for bank runs, if customers lose confidence in the banking system. Central banks and regulatory authorities closely monitor and regulate fractional banking systems to maintain stability and prevent systemic risks.

Fractional banking involves banks keeping only a fraction of customer deposits in reserve while using the remaining funds for lending and other investments. This system allows banks to create money through the process of making loans. Fractional banking, also known as fractional reserve banking, is a banking system in which banks are required to hold only a fraction of customer deposits in reserve.

Fractional Banking:

Frame the Discussion: Initiate a discussion or meeting with your investors specifically focused on competitive analysis. Explain the importance of gaining an external perspective.

Fundraising Strategy: Investors are familiar with the fundraising process. Seek their advice on timing, valuation, and how to present your startup to potential investors.

Global Perspective: If your startup operates internationally or plans to expand globally, investors with international experience can offer insights into regional competitors.

Global Reach: Through technology and the internet, startups can have a global reach from day one. This allows them to access a broader customer base and diverse talent pools.

Gross profit: Revenue minus the costs directly associated with producing goods/services. Does not include overhead, operating, or other indirect costs.

Growth Strategy: Outline your growth strategy, including how you plan to acquire customers, expand into new markets, or launch additional products or services.

Guidance and Expertise: Mentors bring extensive industry knowledge, experience, and expertise to the table. They can offer valuable insights into navigating the challenges and opportunities specific to your startup's industry.

Highlight Key Challenges: Inquire about potential threats or challenges they foresee in the market. This helps you anticipate and prepare for obstacles.

Identify Key Competitors: Discuss who your main competitors are. Investors may offer insights into competitors you might not have considered or competitors emerging in the market.

Identify Target Connections: Clearly communicate your specific networking needs to your investors. Are you looking for potential customers, partners, advisors, or industry experts? Define your target connections.

Identify Your Needs: Start by identifying your specific needs and areas where mentorship can provide the most value. Consider whether you need guidance in areas like business strategy, industry knowledge, leadership skills, or networking.

Identifying opportunities for circular business models and new revenue streams

Ignoring the tax consequences of investments can lead to missed opportunities for tax efficiency. Understanding the tax implications of buying, selling, or holding investments is crucial for maximizing returns.

Impact and Sustainability: If you're focused on social or environmental impact, investors with expertise in impact investing can offer guidance on measuring and maximizing your impact. Refers to a form of investing that seeks to generate positive social and environmental impacts alongside financial returns. The primary goal of impact investing is to address specific societal or environmental challenges while still making profits for investors. This investment approach goes beyond the traditional focus solely on financial gains and emphasizes the importance of creating meaningful and measurable positive outcomes.

Impact of Global Events: Discuss how global events or economic shifts may affect your market. Investors with a global perspective can provide valuable insights into geopolitical risks.

Impact: Entrepreneurs often seek to make a positive impact on society or the environment through their startups. They may focus on sustainability, social causes, or addressing pressing global issues.

Implementation Plan: Develop an implementation plan for strategic changes. Clearly define roles, responsibilities, and timelines to execute the strategy effectively.

Incubators and Accelerators: If your startup is part of an incubator or accelerator program, inquire about mentorship opportunities they may offer. Many of these programs have mentor networks. Organizations that nurture startups in their early stages by providing workspace, seed funding, mentoring, and more in exchange for equity.

Independence: Founders have a degree of independence and control over the direction of the business. They can make strategic decisions without the bureaucracy often found in larger organizations.

Industry Events: Attend industry events, conferences, and networking meetups. These events provide opportunities to meet experienced professionals who could potentially become mentors.

Industry Networking: Ask if your investors are part of industry associations, networks, or forums. Their involvement can provide access to additional market insights and connections.

Industry Trends: Investors stay informed about industry trends. They can help you stay ahead of the curve by providing insights into emerging technologies and market shifts.

Inflation Hedge: Commodities, particularly those like gold, silver, and oil, are often seen as a hedge against inflation. When inflation rises, the prices of commodities tend to increase, potentially providing a counterbalance to the eroding purchasing power of currencies. This can be particularly advantageous during periods of rising inflation.

Innovation and Scalability: Impact investing often encourages innovative solutions that can be scaled up to address broader societal or environmental issues effectively.

Innovation: Financial markets have driven innovation in financial products and technologies, providing new opportunities for investors.

Innovation: Startups are often founded with the goal of bringing new and innovative solutions to the market. They have the flexibility to challenge traditional approaches and disrupt established industries.

Innovations and Trends: Discuss any innovative strategies or emerging trends they see among your competitors. Are there areas where competitors are outpacing you in innovation?

Integration with Strategy: Ensure that the insights gained from this competitive analysis align with your overall business strategy. Use this information to refine your strategic decisions.

Intentionality: Impact investors deliberately direct their capital toward businesses, organizations, or projects that align with their desired social or environmental goals. They actively seek opportunities that can bring about positive change.

Invoice Trading: Platforms that allow businesses to sell their outstanding invoices to investors for immediate cash.

Iterative Strategy: Remember that strategy is not set in stone. It should be flexible and subject to refinement based on changing market conditions and new information.

Job Creation: Startups have the potential to create jobs and stimulate economic growth in their communities. They often hire talent locally and contribute to the local economy.

Keep Investors Informed: Regularly update your investors on the progress of any relationships or partnerships that stem from their introductions. This keeps them engaged and informed.

Key Objectives: Identify the key objectives that will drive your startup's growth and success. These could include revenue targets, market share goals, customer acquisition numbers, or product development milestones.

Lack of Accessibility: Some argue that traditional investing platforms and vehicles are not accessible to all, leading to wealth inequality.

Lack of Transparency: Concerns about transparency exist, especially in areas like private equity and hedge funds, where investors may have limited visibility into the underlying assets.

Lead Investor: The primary investor in a funding round who often sets the terms and conditions for other investors.

Learning Opportunities: The process of building a startup offers continuous learning opportunities. Founders acquire knowledge in areas like product development, marketing, finance, and management.

Legacy Building: Some entrepreneurs are driven by the desire to leave a lasting legacy. They aim to build organizations that outlive them and continue to thrive.

Legal and Compliance: Investors can provide guidance on legal and compliance matters, helping you navigate complex regulations in your industry.

Legal and Governance: Ensure that your objectives and vision align with legal and governance requirements. This is especially important if you have a board of directors or shareholders with voting rights.

Lending and Investment: Banks use the funds from deposits to make loans and investments, thus creating new money in the form of loans.

Leverage LinkedIn: Encourage your investors to use LinkedIn or other professional networking platforms to facilitate introductions. LinkedIn's "Introduction" feature can be especially useful.

Leverage Their Network: Investors often have extensive networks within your industry. Ask them to make introductions to potential partners, customers, or advisors who can help you achieve your strategic goals.

License Fees: Selling or licensing IP, technologies, software, or brand rights that the startup has developed to larger companies in exchange for licensing fees.

Liquidation Preference: A clause in investment agreements that determines the order in which investors receive payouts in the event of a liquidation or exit.

Long-Term Perspective: Mentors often offer a long-term perspective on your startup's journey. They can help you think strategically and plan for sustainable growth.

Long-Term Vision: Discuss your long-term vision with investors. They can offer guidance on how to build a sustainable and scalable business that aligns with your vision. What do they foresee as the future direction, and how can your startup position itself accordingly?

Market Entry Strategies: If you're considering expanding into new markets, ask for advice on market entry strategies. Investors may have insights into the best approaches for entering specific regions or demographics.

Market Entry: Investors with international experience can offer guidance on entering new markets, whether that involves expansion to different regions or countries.

Market Gap: Startups identify market gaps or unmet needs and develop products or services to fill those gaps. This can create a niche in the market and offer a competitive advantage.

Market Insights: Share insights into market conditions, trends, and competitive dynamics. This helps investors understand the external factors affecting your business. Tap into their market insights. Ask for their perspective on market trends, emerging opportunities, and potential threats. This can inform your strategic decisions.

Market Manipulation: Accusations of market manipulation by large institutional investors or high-frequency traders can undermine confidence in the fairness of markets.

Market Opportunity: Clearly articulate the market opportunity your startup is pursuing. This includes the target market, market size, and the specific pain points or needs your solution addresses.

Market Positioning: Seek their input on your market positioning. Are you effectively differentiated from competitors? How is your brand perceived relative to others in the market?

Market Share and Growth: Ask for their views on your market share compared to competitors and their expectations for your future growth relative to the competition.

Market Timing:

Markets and economic conditions change over time. Failing to stay informed about relevant market trends, economic indicators, and changes in regulations can lead to suboptimal investment decisions.

Measurable Impact: Impact investing requires a strong focus on measuring the social and environmental outcomes of the investments. This emphasis on metrics and data helps to ensure accountability and transparency in achieving the intended impact.

Meeting in Person: When possible, meet with key investors in person. Face-to-face interactions can strengthen relationships and provide a deeper understanding of your business.

Mentorship: Some investors are not only interested in providing capital but also in mentoring founders. They can offer advice on leadership, team management, and personal development. Mentorship in the context of a startup refers to a professional relationship in which an experienced individual, known as a mentor, provides guidance, support, and advice to a less experienced entrepreneur or founder, known as a mentee. Mentorship is a valuable resource for startups, offering a range of benefits that can contribute to the growth and success of the business.

Milestones and Achievements: Celebrate key milestones, product launches, partnerships, or significant client wins. These successes showcase your progress and can boost investor confidence.

Mission Statement: Start with a concise mission statement that defines the core purpose of your startup. This statement should answer the question: Why does your startup exist, and what problem does it aim to solve?

Mitigations: Be transparent about the potential risks your startup may face and how you plan to mitigate them. Investors appreciate a well-thought-out risk management strategy. Discuss any potential risks or challenges that could impact your business.

Money Creation: When a customer deposits money in a bank, only a fraction of that deposit is kept in reserve, while the rest is available for the bank to lend.

Multiplier Effect: The process continues as the newly created money is deposited in other banks, allowing them to make additional loans. This has a multiplier effect on the money supply.

Mutual Benefits: Highlight how the mentorship can be mutually beneficial. Mentorship is not just about receiving; it's also an opportunity for mentors to give back and learn from the experience.

Mutually Beneficial: Mentorship is not a one-way street. It can be mutually beneficial as mentors often find satisfaction in helping others succeed and may also learn from their mentees.

MVP (Minimum Viable Product): The most basic version of a product that allows a startup to test its concept and gather user feedback.

Net profit: The total amount left after accounting for all expenses - the company's actual take-home profit. Also referred to as the bottom line.

Network Access: Investors often have extensive networks. They can introduce you to potential customers, partners, and other investors.

Networking Events: Attend industry events, conferences, and meetings where you can meet potential connections in person. Your investors may be able to provide recommendations on events to attend.

Networking Opportunities: Mentors often have extensive networks within the industry. They can introduce you to potential customers, partners, investors, advisors, and other valuable connections.

Networking: Leverage your existing network to identify potential mentors. Reach out to advisors, colleagues, industry contacts, or members of entrepreneurship organizations. They may be able to recommend suitable mentors.

Networking: The startup ecosystem provides opportunities for networking with like-minded individuals, investors, advisors, and potential partners. These connections can be invaluable.

Online Platforms: Explore online mentorship platforms and communities that connect entrepreneurs with experienced mentors. Websites like SCORE, LinkedIn, or industry-specific forums can be valuable resources.

Operating profit (EBIT): Earnings before interest and taxes. Revenue minus overall operating expenses, including overhead, operating costs, depreciation, etc.

OPEX (Operating expense): Ongoing expenditures for operating costs like inventory, marketing, payroll, maintenance, etc.

Peer-to-Peer (P2P) Lending: Platforms that connect borrowers directly with lenders, bypassing traditional financial intermediaries. Platforms like Prosper and Lending Club allow individuals to lend money and charge interest. This cuts banks out of the picture.

Personal Growth: Mentorship can contribute to your personal and professional growth. As you learn from your mentor's experiences, you can become a more effective leader and decision-maker.

Personal Growth: Starting and growing a startup can be a transformative personal journey. It challenges individuals to develop new skills, overcome obstacles, and learn from failures.

Personalized Advice: Mentorship is highly individualized. Mentors tailor their guidance to the specific needs and goals of the startup and its founder. This ensures that the advice is relevant and actionable.

Pitch Deck: A presentation that provides an overview of a startup's business, including its problem statement, solution, market, and financials.

Preferred stock: Ownership shares that may carry additional rights, preferences, or privileges over common shares like dividends, voting, etc.

Pricing Strategies: Inquire about competitors' pricing strategies and how your pricing compares. Investors may have insights into effective pricing models.

Privacy and Confidentiality: Be mindful of privacy and confidentiality concerns when sharing sensitive information. Ensure that you have appropriate safeguards in place.

Problem Solving: Mentors can assist in problem-solving by sharing their experiences and providing alternative perspectives. They may help you identify creative solutions to challenges.

Problem-Solving: Entrepreneurs enjoy the challenge of solving complex problems and overcoming obstacles. Startup founders often encounter a wide range of challenges that test their problem-solving skills.

Product Development: Investors can provide input on product or service development. They may have a deep understanding of customer needs or emerging market trends.

Profit margin: The percentage of profit from total revenue that indicates how profitable the company is.

Progress Tracking: Provide updates on the progress you've made toward your defined objectives and goals. Highlight achievements, milestones reached, and key performance indicators (KPIs).

Q&A Sessions: Consider hosting regular Q&A sessions or conference calls where investors can ask questions and engage in discussions. This fosters interactive communication.

Reach Out: Once you've identified potential mentors, don't hesitate to reach out. Craft a thoughtful and concise message explaining your goals and why you believe they would be a valuable mentor.

Reciprocate When Possible: Be willing to reciprocate by introducing your investors to valuable connections within your own network when appropriate. It's a two-way street.

Recommendations: Encourage your investors to provide recommendations or suggestions based on their competitive analysis. What actions should your startup consider taking?

Regular Updates: Maintain regular communication with your investors. Share updates on your progress, challenges, and strategic initiatives. This ongoing dialogue helps build trust and keeps them engaged in your business.

Regulatory and Compliance: Discuss any regulatory changes or compliance issues that may impact your industry. Investors with regulatory expertise can provide guidance on navigating these challenges. Complex and evolving regulations can create challenges for investors, and some argue that regulatory frameworks may not adequately protect all market participants.

Request Introductions: Ask your investors to make introductions to individuals or organizations within their network who align with your needs. A warm introduction from a trusted source is more likely to yield positive results.

Request Relevant Data: If your investors have access to market data or research reports, ask if they can share relevant information. Data-driven insights can provide a deeper understanding of market trends.

Reserve Requirement: Central banks set a reserve requirement, specifying the percentage of customer deposits that banks must hold in reserve.

Resource Access: Mentors may have access to resources, tools, or information that can benefit your startup, such as market research data or educational materials.

Retirement Planning: Investment vehicles like retirement accounts help individuals plan for their long-term financial security.

Revenue: The total amount of income generated in sales by a company over a specific time period.

Risk Management: Investors often have a keen sense of risk assessment. They can help you identify and mitigate potential risks to your business.

Runway: The amount of time left before a company runs out of cash, given the burn rate and existing funding. Before needing additional capital, it is often measured in months.

Scaling Operations: Investors can provide insights into scaling operations efficiently, including hiring strategies, process improvements, and resource allocation.

Scenario Planning: Collaborate with your investors on scenario planning. Consider various potential futures for the market and develop strategies to thrive under different circumstances.

Scenario Planning: Work with your investors to develop scenarios for different market conditions. This helps you prepare for various eventualities and make agile strategic decisions.

Seed Funding: Initial capital provided to a startup to prove its concept, develop a prototype, or reach a specific milestone. Typically, the founders own financing or capital from family/friends.

Series A, B, C, etc.: Different stages of venture capital financing rounds as a startup matures and seeks additional funding. Series A financing - The first round of financing will be from VC investors once seed funding and a prototype are in place. Companies leverage for growth.

Set Expectations: Be clear about your expectations and what you hope to achieve through the mentorship. Discuss the frequency of meetings, preferred communication methods, and any specific areas of focus.

Short-Term Focus: Critics suggest that there is too much emphasis on short-term gains and trading, which can lead to market volatility and instability.

Skill Development: Mentors can help you develop specific skills or competencies necessary for your role as a founder, such as leadership, decision-making, and negotiation skills.

SMART Goals: Create Specific, Measurable, Achievable, Relevant, and Time-bound (SMART) goals.

These are clear, quantifiable objectives that guide your startup's actions and decisions.

Socially Responsible Investing: The rise of socially responsible and sustainable investing allows investors to align their values with their investment choices.

Stay Organized: Use a CRM (Customer Relationship Management) system or another organizational tool to keep track of your networking efforts, conversations, and follow-ups.

Strategic Initiatives: Discuss any strategic initiatives or changes in your business plan. Explain the rationale behind these decisions and how they align with your long-term vision.

Strategy: Provide your investors with insight into your business strategy, including your goals and objectives. This helps them understand how their network connections can contribute to your success.

Strengths and Weaknesses: Ask your investors to assess your startup's strengths and weaknesses compared to competitors. What do they see as your competitive advantages? Where do you face challenges?

Team Updates: Highlight any changes or additions to your team. Emphasize the skills and experience new team members bring to the organization.

Technology Tools: Utilize technology tools such as email newsletters, investor portals, or collaboration platforms to streamline communication and document sharing.

Term Sheet: A non-binding document outlining the key terms and conditions of an investment, including valuation, equity stake, and investor rights.

Timely Response: Respond promptly to inquiries or concerns raised by investors. Timely and respectful communication demonstrates professionalism.

Unicorn: A startup with a valuation exceeding $1 billion.

Validation and Confidence: Having a respected mentor can provide validation for your startup's vision and strategy. This validation can boost your confidence and credibility, especially when seeking investment.

Valuation: An estimate of the overall economic value of a business used to set sale/investment prices. Common methods include discounted cash flows, comparables, and assets-based approaches. The estimated worth of a startup is usually determined during funding rounds.

Venture Capital (VC): Capital invested by firms that fund startups and small businesses with high growth potential. Typically, larger amounts are invested in later stages.VC firms invest substantial sums of money into high-growth potential startups in exchange for equity. VCs offer guidance as well as capital. Professional investment firms that pool money from various sources to invest in startups and early-stage companies.

Vesting: A process by which founders or employees earn their equity over time, typically with a one- to four-year vesting period.

Vision Statement: Develop a vision statement that outlines your long-term aspirations. This should describe the impact you want your startup to have on the world or your industry in the future.

Volatility: Commodities are known for their price volatility, which can result in significant fluctuations in the value of the fund. Sudden supply and demand imbalances, geopolitical factors, and global economic conditions can impact commodity prices, leading to substantial gains or losses.

Wealth Creation: Investing has been a historically significant wealth creator, allowing individuals and institutions to grow their assets over time.

Working capital: A measure of a company's liquidity and overall efficiency. Calculated as current assets minus current liabilities and debt.

References

Here's a list of references. These references cover various aspects of startup financing, venture capital, entrepreneurial finance, and related topics.

Bhide, A. (1992). Bootstrap finance: The art of startups. *Harvard Business Review, 70*(6), 109117

Cumming, D., & Johan, S. (2013). *Venture capital and private equity contracting: An international perspective.* Academic Press.

Ewens, M., & Malenko, N. (2022). The benefits of friends in venture capital: Evidence from the U.S. startup ecosystem. *Journal of Financial Economics,* 146(1), 119.

Gompers, P., & Lerner, J. (2001). The venture capital revolution. *Journal of Economic Perspectives*, 15(2), 145168.

Gornall, W., & Strebulaev, I. A. (2020). Squaring venture capital valuations with reality. *Journal of Financial Economics*, 135(1), 120144.

Hellmann, T., & Puri, M. (2000). The interaction between product market and financing strategy: The role of venture capital. *Review of Financial Studies*, 13(4), 959984.

Kaplan, S. N., & Strömberg, P. (2003). Financial contracting theory meets the real world: An empirical analysis of venture capital contracts. *Review of Economic Studies*, 70(2), 281315.

Metrick, A., & Yasuda, A. (2010). The economics of private equity funds. *Review of Financial Studies*, 23(6), 23032341.

Rajan, R. G. (2012). Presidential address: The corporation in finance. *Journal of Finance*, 67(4), 11731217.

Ritter, J. R. (1991). The longrun performance of initial public offerings. *Journal of Finance,* 46(1), 327.

Sahlman, W. A. (1990). The structure and governance of venture capital organizations. *Journal of Financial Economics*, 27(2), 473521.

Stuart, T. E., & Sorenson, O. (2007). Strategic networks and entrepreneurial ventures. *Strategic Entrepreneurship Journal*, 1(34), 211227.

Tirole, J. (2006). *The theory of corporate finance*. Princeton University Press.

Zider, B. (1998). How venture capital works. *Harvard Business Review*, 76(6), 131139.

Zingales, L. (1998). Survival of the fittest or the fattest? Exit and financing in the trucking industry. *Journal of Finance*, 53(3), 905938.

This list includes seminal works and recent studies that would be relevant and useful for readers of The Broken Line interested in understanding the complexities of finance in the startup environment.

www.ingramcontent.com/pod-product-compliance
Lightning Source LLC
LaVergne TN
LVHW020018170826
845678LV00001B/29
9798895253335